Traditional Architecture

Traditional Architecture

Timeless Building for the Twenty-First Century

Alireza Sagharchi and Lucien Steil

Foreword by HRH The Prince of Wales
Preface by Léon Krier

RIZZOLI
NEW YORK

New York · Paris · London · Milan

First published in the United States of America
in 2013 by Rizzoli International Publications, Inc.
300 Park Avenue South
New York, NY 10010
www.rizzoliusa.com

ISBN: 978-0-8478-4080-9
LCCN: 2013946644

Designed by Beatriz Cifuentes

Distributed to the U.S. trade by Random House,
New York

Printed and bound in China

2013 2014 2015 2016 2017 / 10 9 8 7 6 5 4 3 2 1

Acknowledgments

We would like to express our gratitude to all those who were instrumental in making this publication possible. Our thanks to Dr. David Watkin for encouragement and advice when we first discussed the idea for the book during the 2011 Driehaus Award Ceremony in Chicago. We owe a very heartfelt thanks to David Morton, Associate Publisher for Architecture at Rizzoli, for his enthusiastic and generous support and guidance. Our thanks also to Douglas Curran and Ron Broadhurst, at Rizzoli, and Beatriz Cifuentes for their craftsmanship and excellence in editing our manuscript and designing a book of the highest quality.

Our thanks to Rose Belderbos and Amy Spraggs for taking on the monumental task of coordinating and collating all the material and liaising with the architects across four continents.

We are grateful to the Aga Khan Foundation and Farrokh Derakhshani, director of the Aga Khan Award for Architecture, for giving us access to a wealth of material and for allowing us to publish the work of their laureates, and to the University of Notre Dame School of Architecture and Dean Michael Lykoudis for providing material from their Driehaus Prize laureates.

Our eternal gratitude goes to His Royal Highness the Prince of Wales for writing the foreword to the book and for his support of a sustainable, ecological global project encompassing the timeless achievements of contemporary classical and traditional architecture. HRH The Prince of Wales has been the most ardent supporter of a growing contemporary movement of traditional architecture and urbanism through the work of The Prince's Foundation for Building Community and the International Network for Traditional Building, Architecture, and Urbanism (INTBAU).

Our thanks go to all the fellow architects, in practice or academy, from across the globe who with generosity of spirit supported our effort and inspired this long overdue book with their built and unbuilt projects over the last decades.

And thanks go to Mina and Nima Sagharchi, Laura and Jim Steil, and Aiko Riceputi-Steil for their enthusiastic support and encouragement.

Table of Contents

CLARENCE HOUSE

Modern civilization began when people started to live together in communities which then became villages and, in turn, towns and cities. Architecture and urbanism were not far behind. For centuries, we lived in harmony with Nature, which is fundamental to the relationship of humans to their environment. Architecture helps to define us as human beings, and to symbolize the way we look at the world. It affects our psychological well-being, and can either enhance or detract from our sense of community We are profoundly influenced by it; by the presence, or absence, of beauty and harmony, which I believe lie at the heart of genuine sustainability.

Over the past century, Modernist planning and urban design have literally fragmented and deconstructed the world into a series of "zoned" parts, without any sensible order such as occurs in Nature. How and what we build has become a process wholly detached from local traditions and cultural identity, let alone from Nature, as though we have decided consciously to work against our environment as part of some gigantic, uncontrolled experiment.

However, today, the re-birth of the New Traditional Architecture in Great Britain and continental Europe, coupled with the New Urbanism movement in the United States, has at last started influencing the way we shape our buildings and neighbourhoods. A return to a traditional pattern of streets in new urban centres, building with natural and sustainable materials and the re-use of time-honoured skills and techniques alongside the best of contemporary technology, offers an alternative to throwing the baby out with the bathwater. I am delighted to say that both my Institute of Architecture, and my Foundation for Building Community, were instrumental in this movement at a time when such ideas were deeply unpopular.

The exemplary projects in this book, brought together by Alireza Sagharchi and Lucien Steil, show us the emergence and rebirth of a vibrant and sustainable culture of building worldwide, whose identity is strongly rooted in local culture. New Traditional Architecture is in a unique position to be able to respond to contemporary needs in vastly different parts of the world. This marriage of universal principles with local adaptation connects, for instance, a bamboo school building in Dinajpur, Bangladesh, to my own development in Poundbury and the Ciudad Cayala development designed by Leon Krier in Guatemala.

I do believe most strongly that the values which underpin the New Traditional Architecture – namely the importance of passing on knowledge, skills and cultural continuity – are ideas held by people and societies around the globe. We have a duty of care to Nature and community to preserve and honour these values which are fundamental to our legacy, to the survival of our built heritage and to the ultimate wellbeing of future generations in an overcrowded and resource-constrained world.

Traditional Architecture

Not a Historical but a Technological Heritage

Léon Krier

Many people reject the possibility of traditional architecture today because of a crass categorical misunderstanding. They amalgamate architectural with mythological traditions. They confuse empirical know-how with metaphysical speculation. They erroneously equate building technology with transcendental belief systems.

Traditional architectural forms are shaped by man's enduring use of natural building materials to adequately settle in specific climates and geographic and cultural conditions. They make up part of the timeless technological heritage of man. They are as permanently relevant to the welfare of humans as common languages, tools, vehicles, science, and techniques. To declare them as being mere historical heritage and therefore past and dated phenomena is not only a philosophic mistake but an ideologically motivated error calling for authoritative correction.

Over centuries traditional architectures around the world have evolved a great variety of building languages. Unlike spoken languages, the elements constituting the traditional building vocabulary need no translation in order to be understood across borders and ages. Of universal validity, they are part of technology before and beyond (transcending) mere historical deployments and meanings.

As the buildings published in this tome demonstrate, modern traditional builders or designers are naturally polyglot, can within no time decipher and master local idioms, and realize structures in harmony with local traditions, culture, climate, soil, altitude. This cultural and technical versatility singularly contrasts with the dumb and blind modernist monoglotism, imposing the same building types and mannerism across the planet, irrespective of culture, climate, or geography. To build traditionally today is not ignoring the demands of modern life, on the contrary it demands a challenging intellectual and professional determination, often against overwhelming peer pressures, bureaucratic chicanery, reigning fashionable fads, and, most determinant, the pervading tyrannical impositions of a large-scale construction industry and its powerful pro-regulations lobbies.

Pages 10–13: Redevelopment of Tor Bella Monaca, Rome
Architects Léon Krier, Cristiano Rosponi, and Jamshid Sepehri

Modernism upholds the idea that industrialization and the technological revolutions irreversibly changed all conceptions of life and hence of building and settling the earth—that we have no choice in the matter, that we must submit to the paradigmatic shift, that its refusal is condemning us to anachronism, ridicule, and oblivion. "You are bypassed by history," Phyllis Lambert whistled in my ear on the occasion of the Eisenman-Krier exhibition at the Yale School of Architecture.

The buildings published in this book are designed by architects who are unimpressed by modernist calls to order. They disobey consciously the siren song they were deafened with in colleges and universities. For most of them doing the right thing for a lifetime has earned them little professional recognition and no institutional glory.

How can this scandalous behavior be explained? Are they off their minds, have they lost their senses? Or is there a rational justification for what is at best brushed aside as a romantic, irrelevant rebellion?

Poundbury Queen's Square Tower
Architect Léon Krier

There is now a broad consciousness growing of the fact that modernist architecture and suburbanism are uniquely dependent on the massive and sustained availability of fossil fuels. Modernism is not a paradigmatic, irreversible historical phenomenon; on the contrary, the Leviathan, fed on slave labor and for two centuries raised to monstrous proportions on hydrocarbons, will literally run out of fuel. It is an epiphenomenon of the recently peaked fossil fuel age, the consequence of which the world economy is now resizing itself to. Within a generation from now megasized buildings, sprawling suburbs, and synthetic materials may become items only affordable by privileged and hyper-militarized minorities, and the traditional architectures illustrated in this book may be the first blossoms of a massive trend reversal.

"There is no going back," the routine battle cry, needs urgent revision. If we fully obeyed the imperative, we would of necessity have to reject experience itself. The use of languages and tools demonstrate a permanent going back to an immemorial past. Why should architecture and the arts be subjected to an insane moralist injunction which science, technology, and language, in fact human behaviors and nature itself, so generally disobey.

The slogan "There is no going back" reveals in my opinion two fundamental fears of modern man. The fear of aging and the fear of backwardness are destroying right now more of mankind's architectural and urban heritage than natural catastrophes and wars. The worldwide rape of traditional buildings and environs by jarring forms, inappropriate materials, colors, and uses, is in my opinion motivated by the same "fear" that impels people to have bodies and souls disfigured by operations of rejuvenation. Beware of the consequences when surgeons, like contemporary "fine artists," become more driven by zeitgeist concern than by classical models and aesthetics.

To eat, to wash, to walk, to drive, to write, to speak, to live are imitative activities. Without permanent repetition, imitation, reconstruction, and reproduction according to type, the planet is within a generation turned into a cemetery of its former self. Imitation is the fundamental principle of life. Where there is life there is "permanent going back" to things experienced and past; there is no present nor future possible otherwise. In fact what ecology is now ineluctably teaching is that there is "no more going forward" on fossil fuels without a horrendous price to be paid. Those who can't go backward shouldn't stop those who can.

Technical colleges and universities around the world commonly not only refuse to teach traditional forms of urbanism, architecture, and building but, ranging them with art history, they actively deny their technological or artistic legitimacy. The expansion of the ecological imperatives and conscience will lead to an inevitable resurgence of traditional techniques and their dominance over historicist/modernist ideologies.

A de-ideologized building technology, be it high, medium, or low tech, encompasses all building materials, natural or artificial, according to their specificity, and in the long term it is their ecological price that will decide whether a building material, technique, language, or type is traditional and therefore modern or obsolete, and therefore "historical" and dated. There is absolutely no reason why some modernist ideas could not be integrated into the body of traditional architecture. The flat roof and the inclined roof, the curtain wall and the load-bearing wall, the vertical and the horizontal window, are not, as modernists pretend, ideological opponents or contradictions but different techniques of roofing, constructing, sealing, and lighting buildings.

The nightmare scenarios for the future are ethnic sectarianism at one extreme and leveling of cultural and geographical differences on the other. The only certainty is that there will not be a single global architectural style. It is contrary to reason and ecology. Espousing traditional architecture and urbanism should not be an ideological but an intellectual decision, not lead by an emotional but a rational intent.

What is now a mere intellectual and personal choice will very soon become a collective necessity; the earlier we recognize the overwhelming trend, the better for our cities, buildings, and citizens. For the skeptics I add that even if "peak oil" were by some miracle to be delayed into an unfathomable future, there are overwhelming reasons for our own sake and sanity to return to the human-scale traditional building methods, architecture, and urbanism so convincingly demonstrated around the world by this book.

Introduction

Alireza Sagharchi and Lucien Steil

There is nothing past for which one may yearn, there is only an eternal newness which is shaped by the wider elements of the past and true nostalgia has always to be productive to create a new excellence.

J. W. von Goethe

The *New Palladians* exhibition of 2008 at the Prince's Foundation for Building Community, and the subsequent publication of the book *New Palladians: Modernity and Sustainability for 21st Century Architecture*, led to the realization that the book only touched upon a fragment of a remarkable phenomena that we have personally been involved with over the last thirty years. Classicism and a creative culture of traditional architecture and urbanism have been reemerging, blossoming, and successfully expanding far beyond a simple state of resilience. Some twenty years ago it was almost impossible to list any significant output apart from essays, drawings, and counterproposals from this new generation of architects. We now have a great number of practitioners and craftsmen all over the world designing and building a contemporary architecture inspired by the intelligence, sustainability, and excellence of traditional architecture and urbanism. These architects skillfully operate within a wider and pluralistic refreshed building tradition, articulating their knowledge and expertise of both classical and vernacular architecture. They successfully continue the legacy of the early twentieth century, of masters like Jože Plečnik, John Russell Pope, François Spoerry, Frank Lloyd Wright, Philip Trammell Shutze, Hassan Fathy, Raymond Erith, Geoffrey Bawa, and Pierre Barbe and are inspired by the present-day generation of thinkers and practitioners led by Rob and Léon Krier, Maurice Culot, Robert Adam, Quinlan Terry, Christopher Alexander, Robert A. M. Stern, Demetri Porphyrios, David Watkin, Vincent Scully, and Carroll William Westfall. Not surprisingly modern classicism and contemporary traditional architecture and urbanism have shown endurance, longevity, and validity, and above all a growing popularity and success. Traditional practitioners have clearly found a validation as a vital and creative part of contemporary architectural production and have grown influential again in academy and theory.

In this context, when selecting the projects for this book, it seemed prudent to reconsider the whole perspective of what it means to practice as a traditional architect in the twenty-first century. At the same time it became obvious that some strands of thought running through the work of the "New Palladians" emerged as a recurring theme. The inclusion of a substantial body of work from non-Western, North American, European, and Latin American countries was not only rewarding in terms of quality and diversity but symptomatic of a paradigm shift in the assessment of "world architecture" as a fundamental and vital asset of a global architectural ecosystem. The endeavor led to the emergence of universalities, similarities, and generalities that span a global building culture independent of its geographical location or culture and at the same time acknowledge local particularities and contrasts. The idea of a vernacular-classical dialogue was adopted as a fundamental guiding thread of the book's architectural journey as we believe this dialogue transcends both the general and the particular to reveal the true, real, and authentic. Léon Krier's statement on the nature of this relationship sums up this dialogue:

Vernacular building is necessarily linked to geo-climatic conditions and/or local material. A regional style represents the culture of forms and techniques suitable for a region suitable to its climate, material and topographic conditions. Its aesthetic and character emerge from the infinitely varied intelligent repeating of basic, continuously adapted formal typological inventory. Classical (Traditional architecture) architecture develops transregional, universal styles. Even though its elements are anchored in the vernacular of a region (Tuscan, Doric, Ionian ...) or in the style of an era, dynasty or ruler, their elaborate and symbolic codification transcend both place and period and lend themselves to continual or even universal implementation ...

The projects assembled here highlight the awareness of a sustainable *localism* and the continuity of traditional building crafts on a global scale and reveal the resilience and originality of traditional building cultures despite enormous economic and cultural pressures of contemporary development. It is also interesting to note the emergence of new transcultural synergies between Western and non-Western professionals, inhabitants, organizations, and populace in the form of an inspiring and fertile type of "fair trade" in architecture. This has replaced former models of cultural colonialism with the establishment of architectural awards such as the Aga Khan or the Driehaus Prize. The idea of a positive "globalization" combined with the renaissance of traditional building arts and crafts articulated in a dialogue from vernacular to classical makes an extraordinarily compelling argument. Concepts of meaningful development and historical culture have survived and become resilient to the impact of industrial modernization, mass tourism, kitsch, and the caricatured folkloric icons of modernism on a global scale. In an age of pluralism, democratic processes are being introduced in every walk of life in new and emerging social structures and established sophisticated cultures, based on inclusive social, cultural, and economic resources being more fairly and democratically distributed. In architecture, the dominance of an anti-tradition bias by an architectural establishment and its monopoly of education is probably one of the last vestiges of a previous century where hegemony of a dominant ideology was the modus operandi. On the other hand the natural and intrinsic pluralism of traditional cultures with their dialogue between vernacular and classical supports democratic and participative processes, community building and empowerment, civic engagement and creativity.

Another visible stand of the selected projects is the fertile interaction between vernacular and classical architectures. The vernacular is often rooting the architecture within the contingencies of the territory, with the geography, climate, resources, skills, and culture of a place. The classical, on the other hand, introduces a cosmopolitan and delocalized paradigm, transcending cultures while responding to specificities of a particular cultural context. For emerging countries classicism signifies a search for an architectural language that exemplifies local/national expression, akin to the national romantic movement in Sweden at the turn of the twentieth century. There the search was for an indigenous language of architecture that would express a particularly Swedish modernity and put the nation's culture in the global context; the movement, named Swedish Grace, resulted in a prolific and wonderful inventory of building and the emergence of architects like Gunnar Asplund and Sigurd Lewerentz. On the other hand, the emergence of classicism in the highly developed Western European and North American countries is about reengaging with a language and technique of construction lost through rampant industrialization, a language that allows the vernacular and the classical built environment of a culture to both serve the local identity and its global aspirations.

Another remarkable feature that we endeavored to encompass is the concept of "micro-projects." These are often made up of buildings and their immediate context, or a smaller grouping of buildings with courtyards or gardens, in contrast to large urban ensembles or "macro-developments." Supporting organic and incremental growth and change over time, they allow participatory processes, local involvement, medium and microfinancing, better contextual and environmental integration, and ecological viability. Avoiding the pitfalls of "grand projects," they are proportional and scalar interventions that can be organically developed and built in a context of complexity and continuity. They refer to traditional precedents, types, and patterns that favor identity, continuity, and permanence, as well as adaptive change and sustainable modernity. This "other modernity" has replaced an industrialized pastiche and become a global phenomenon, particularly in deprived parts of the world, restating an ecological and cultural aspiration for difference, variety, and complexity based on intelligent choices, inspired visions, and the pursuit of happiness rather than on subjective artistic and intellectual experimentations.

Analogies and parallels also emerged with the early modern movement and early Bauhaus, which was inspired by an interest in crafts and tectonics as well as animated by a social agenda and humanism. The heartfelt and rational urge to reclaim an architecture which is logical, organic, and symbolically relevant, an architecture "which is of its time and universal," as Hassan Fathy stated, is still relevant today. The making of things and buildings in local, natural, healthy materials according to the natural laws of gravity and ecology is very much in the spirit of the classical Vitruvian principles of "Commoditas, Firmitas, Venustas." Materials and methods follow processes of assemblage and construction by means of architecture, such as *poesis*, of making and "imitation of nature" where architecture rivals nature, in order not to replace but to emulate and enhance the synergies of the man-made and of the natural, to create a sustainable built environment in harmonious equilibrium with nature.

The works presented in the book are also "modern" in the positive acknowledgment of the contemporary and of its relevance while avoiding mere obsession with modernity. The originality of the "modern" can only be meaningfully understood and assessed if preceding traditions and historic cultures are also acknowledged and assumed as integral parts of the human space-time condition. Mediated through this modernity, they demonstrate maturity and patina as well as a permanence and newness. They embody memory, intelligence, and imagination; they enhance life, beauty, and comfort and can accommodate change and growth in a perspective of continuity and ecological responsibility.

The idea of newness compels a natural urge for updating, adapting, and regenerating, which contribute to keeping traditions sustainable and exciting. Every culture and society strives to perfect and enhance its traditions and common values and eventually manage change. In a historical context, change is often a succession of discrete corrections and adjustments over time and rarely a radical transformation. It also is important to distinguish the difference between "newness" and "novelty." For this we need to understand the original meaning of tradition from the Latin *tradere*, meaning "handing over" an accumulated, selected, and time-tested wisdom and know-how from one generation to another, not as a frozen doctrine but as a gift of genius to carefully and responsibly nurture, enrich, and perfect.

Contrary to current architectural trends, which are perpetuated and often immediately redundant by the search for yet another "novelty," new aesthetics, and innovations, the projects in this book demonstrate the inventiveness and dexterity of architects who practice globally. Immersed in other traditions or contexts, traditional architects and urbanists confidently tackle problems of building in a particular region and find solutions in the genius of the locality and universality of classicism. This process of sensitive local intervention utilizing existing typology, technology, and elements of architecture also leads to new compositions, inventions, and innovations. This dexterity of approach allows the new buildings to survive in a locality, which makes them timeless, embedded in the building culture of a place, in their time, and in the awareness of a wider world. As Hassan Fathy noted in *Natural Energy and Vernacular Architecture: Principles and Examples with Reference to Hot Arid Climates*:

If we are to reconcile time with the architect's definition of contemporaneity, we must say that to be "relevant to its time," to be "contemporary," a work of architecture must fulfill these conditions: it must be part of the bustle and turmoil, the ebb and flow of everyday life; it must be related harmoniously to the rhythm of the universe; and it must be consonant with man's current stage of knowledge of change. Every journey enlightens, enriches, and is conducive to greater understanding so that we may benefit from the experience in the greater journey of human habitation and environmental stewardship of the globe.

Our architectural journey from the vernacular to the classical presented us with an optimistic vision of a new breed of traditional architects who possess the necessary knowledge, understanding, and tools to enrich the future we intend to inhabit and acknowledge the past we have learned from.

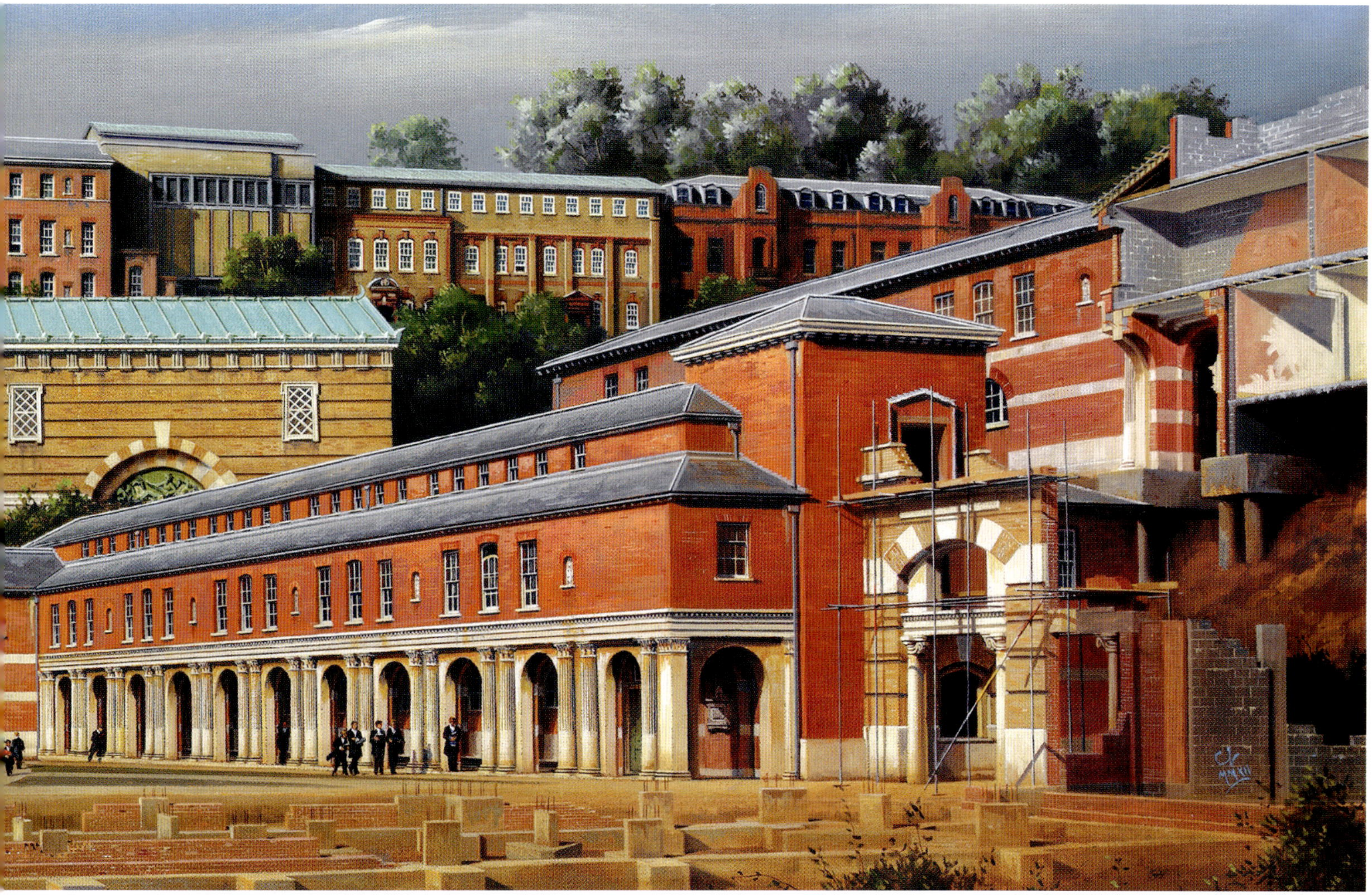

Capriccio *of John Simpson Architects' new quadrangle and buildings for Eton College. Painting by Carl Lambin*

Modern Traditional Architecture

Notes on an Intellectual Lineage

Samir Younés

After the collection of facts, the search for causes.

Hippolyte Taine

Ideas and forms compel their adherents to trace their beginnings, their development, transformation, migration, ruination, or their reemergence—in a word, their lineage. Intellectual lineage is one of the most fervently debated questions among modern traditional architects. One half of this question concerns not only how far back in history this lineage can be traced, both in terms of schools of thought and in terms of individual architects, but how far back it *should* be traced. The other half consists in speculating about what might be the future directions of this intellectual lineage. There is a diffused belief among architects, especially in the United States, that the period broadly known as postmodernism, in culture at large and in architecture in particular, partially opened the way to the practice of traditional architecture. Others specify that only one part of postmodernism, represented by architects who entertained classicizing tendencies, can reasonably be related to modern traditional architecture. Other architects, by contrast, emphasize that modern traditional architecture as a system that rationally links the urban, the architectural, and the tectonic scales evolved from ideas and forms that have little or nothing to do with postmodernism. It is true that modern traditional architecture and postmodernism evolved at the same time. Simultaneity, however, might imply mutual influence but not necessarily unity of principles, forms, and purpose.

Léon Krier, Tor Bella Monaca

That modern traditional architecture includes plural expressions can be explained by the fact that it emerged from various cultural contexts; it has had several beginnings. Yet both its rise and development have received less attention on the part of architectural historians than those of postmodernism. In fact, architectural historians with modernist convictions have either disingenuously disregarded modern traditional architecture or rapidly condemned it with a sleight of hand. This is why traditional architects (sometimes referring to themselves as "The Other Modern") rightly lament the lack of a comprehensive history of their collective work and firmly oppose certain historical methods and conclusions.[1] Where modernist historiography emphasized a view of architectural history based on stylistic rupture and transgression, one period inexorably replacing the previous one, traditional architects seek to uphold continuities or rather the continuity of what has rationally been proven successful in architecture. They affirm respect and even reverence to great architectural traditions. They hasten to explain that modern traditional architecture and urbanism is the convergence of several strands within architecture that go back to the mid-1950s, to the 1920s, and much earlier. Some traditional architects even wish to see an unbroken continuity going back to the Renaissance. Their list is varied and broad and includes: 1) the rational strategies aimed at reconstructing architecture and the city evolving since the 1970s and 1980s; 2) the classicizing architecture that was practiced in the former Soviet Union well into the 1960s; 3) the period rich in traditional architecture spanning between the two World Wars in Italy, Spain, the United States, and many other countries; 4) the period of the fin-de-siècle with its broad, whimsical, and sometimes confused eclecticism; 5) the radical classicism of the early nineteenth century; 6) the sharp rationalism of the architecture of the Enlightenment; 7) the remarkable integration of architectural forms known as the Renaissance; and beyond.

But although traditional architectural knowledge may be rooted in several enduring traditions that can be revived and revised, modern traditional architecture did grow out of specific historical conditions—most particularly out of an intense intellectual revolt against the devastation of cities and the countryside in the postwar years. The monistic practices of modernism, the destruction of nature and the city by the supposedly irrevocable demands of progress, the deep psychological costs of urban blightedness, the reduction of culture and architectural culture into sets of consumable products, or the symbolic poverty of contemporary art and architecture; all of these phenomena could only provoke and justify their reversal: the institution of pluralist practices, the reconstruction of the city based on enduring urban and architectural forms, linking enduring ecological practices with the poetic (or poietic, from the Greek *poiesis*, to make) refinement of construction into tectonics, and the unapologetic desire for the beautiful, for the humane, for the clear sense of place, and for redeeming the devastating loss that has plagued the city.

Operative Precedents

By their very working methods traditional architects associate practice with intellectual lineage, drawing upon multiple strands of architectural expression, on their history and theory in relation to larger cultural currents. After all, tradition at its best requires the uses of practical reason in daily work and in the judicious selection of precedents. Practice and precedence reciprocally form each other. But in weaving their narratives, in their choice of sequential historical links, traditional architects are not immune to the seduction of teleological arguments. If they correctly criticize the determinist narrative according to which modernist architecture happened as if by necessity (historicism), then they themselves might benefit from the same criticism. For in their well-intentioned zeal to attract and include sympathetic positions some traditional architects have hastily incorporated into their narrative some unconvincing and at times ambiguous antecedents. The fact that some architects, architectural theorists, and a handful of architectural historians opposed modernism and discredited its tenets does not necessarily make them forthright supporters of traditional architecture. Some were instrumental in debunking modernist ideology while simultaneously maintaining their admiration of modernist forms. Others still delighted in residing midway between traditional cultures and modernist culture while at once appreciating and condemning parts of each. Expressing sympathy toward some form of tradition—as some postmodernists did—does not necessarily lead to traditional architecture as if it were an ineluctable linear sequence. Nor is the mere toleration of traditional architecture within a pluralistic context also an expression of support.

By way of illustration, it is one thing to say that Robert Venturi (b. 1925) wished to introduce a mannerist "complexity and contradiction" into architecture through compositional analogies drawn from Italian Baroque and Mannerist architecture, but it is another to claim him as one of the precursors of modern traditional architecture. For his joint project with Denise Scott Brown (b. 1931) to move architecture into the semiotic sphere implied—in their case—an architecture transformed into one of the signs of mass advertising displayed by the consumer society. It is one thing to say that Colin Rowe (1920–1999), beginning in the late 1950s, did much to debunk modernism and express a keen interest in urban contextualism, in the lessons of the traditional city, or in Renaissance architectural composition, but it is another to say that he would have championed modern traditional architecture even if he would have encouraged it as an irritant to the cult of the *zeitgeist*. It is one thing to extol the valuable writings of Aldo Rossi (1931–1997) on urban typologies, on the idea of autonomous architecture, urban memory, and the analogous city, and another to contend that had he lived longer he might have taken the decisive step to become a traditional architect. Some of Rossi's buildings exhibit a cautious approach that poetically evokes some of the enduring images of tradition while stopping short of becoming traditional architecture. He certainly had the knowledge and capacity to produce traditional architecture but he never wished to completely sever his ties to modernism. And yet relevant parts of these individuals' work—to mention only three among many as we shall see—played a useful role in furnishing later architects with some of the intellectual material needed to take the next logical and decisive step toward traditional architecture. This is not to reproach the earlier architects for lacking the courage to embrace traditional architecture, rather, to give due value to their intellectual choices, which were frequently met with professional and academic hostility.

These brief examples bring to the fore two related intellectual activities: 1) justifying the bases of modern traditional architecture, and 2) tracing its lineage. Both tasks are vitally entwined in the intellectual life of traditional architects because they connect justificatory principles with historical sequences of particular significance. Modern traditional architecture has been developing a comprehensive system for dwelling wisely on this planet on ecological, urban, and architectural levels, or as Léon Krier (b. 1946) calls it a reconstruction project. Writing the present intellectual lineage of modern traditional architecture, incomplete though it is, concerns the linking of ideas and forms that led to the elaboration and cohering of this international reconstruction project by the mid- to late 1980s. Herein lies a significant concern for methodology. An earlier event may play a meaningful role in the formation of a later event, but mere antecedence does not necessarily establish causality. In other words, a *useful antecedent* is not the same as a genuinely *operative precedent*. Architects who build a system of ideas make connections to previous intellectual strands, but that does not mean that those who came earlier would have wanted these connections to the same degree. Linking ideas and forms belongs more to those who come later. These are some of the sensibilities involved in narrating the conditions of a presently evolving, multicentric, and multicultural traditional architecture that now counts three generations.

Reason, Urban Form, and Architectural Types.

In 1959 Modenese architect and historian Saverio Muratori (1910–1973) published a seminal study concerning the urban evolution of Venice: *Studi per una operante storia urbana di Venezia*. The purpose of this ten-year study,[2] was to produce accurate plans for all of Venice's quarters, including all the buildings, streets, and squares (*campi*), and to provide assumptions regarding their earlier developments since the eighth and ninth centuries. Muratori combined socio-historical scholarship with an architectural typological analysis that

Top right: Saverio Muratori, Plan of Quartiere di San Bartolomio, Venice, Italy, 1959

Top left: Saverio Muratori, San Giovanni at Catano, Pisa, Italy, 1947

Above: Arduino Cantàfora, Cittá Analoga, *1973*

aimed specifically at understanding the urban continuity of the city in relation not only to her architectural characters but also to the problems of growth that became increasingly more acute since the nineteenth century. He hoped that his approach would provide a counterpoint to the prevalent positivist methods of planning cities in the 1950s. In studying the urban history of Venice, Muratori and his collaborators concluded that 1) architectural types find their embodiments within the urban fabric, and that 2) the urban fabric, in turn, has its embodiment in the whole urban form as a totality, the "urban organism" in his words, and 3) that the total value of the urban organism is only grasped through its intrinsic historical continuity.[3] Muratori's analysis showed that one of the gravest problems that beleaguered contemporary cities under the influence of modernism derived, in part, from the abstract consideration of buildings as objects that are isolated from the urban fabric. By contrast, his analyses of Venice, and later the Campo Marzio in Rome, showed how the structuralizing influence of urban form (streets, squares, and blocks) helped to modify building types and characters and anchor them to a place.[4]

Muratori's analyses placed less emphasis on a linear historical, and causal, development of Venice. Rather, it demonstrated how urban morphology and building typology mutually or, rather, dialectically transformed each other and reinforced each other. And this urban dialectic in Venice could only have matured through reasoned reciprocal transformations assured by an urban continuity that spanned many generations. Yet, this was precisely what modernist ideology had been trying to prevent in its emphasis on rupture and transgression of previous traditions, its uncoupling of imitation from invention, and its replacement of the city by a multitude of object-buildings inhabiting a ubiquitous, undefined, and uncontained space. Although Muratori's pedagogy put into direct comparison the layered lessons of Venice's long history in contrast to the crises facing contemporary cities, it is important to note that he did not directly propose that the results of his historical analytical method be turned into a strategy for present-day practice.[5] Nonetheless, while he offered a gentle critique of the current teaching and practice of architecture, it is also quite significant that some of Muratori's buildings were definitely moving in a traditional direction as seen, for example, in his 1947 Chiesa Parrocchiale di San Giovanni al Catano in Pisa, and other projects such as his 1955 Sede del Partito Democratico, Palazzo Sturzo, in Rome.[6]

Architects and historians who studied the rich architectural layers of traditional cities and their varied characters were compelled to identify with precision the urban and architectural elements that assured certain undeniable continuities and contributed to the idea of locus, the sense of place. One of these enduring elements is the concept of type, which was reintroduced into the architectural discourse in the early 1960s by Torinese art historian Giulio Carlo Argan (1909–1992) and the *Casabella* group based, in part, on the formative concept of type articulated by French theorist Antoine-Chrysostôme Quatremère de Quincy (1755–1849). Argan discussed type as a formal resemblance between a class of buildings that can be called, in his words, a "root form." However, contrary to Quatremère's Platonic concept of type as an a priori principle, Argan's typology is a deduction based on observations in a series, on direct formal analogies.[7] Quatremère's distinction between type as "the idea of an element that must serve as a rule for the model" and his understanding of the model "in the sense of practical execution" as a precise building example are tied to another distinction: that of the imitation from the copy.[8] The copy, for Quatremère, implies an identical repetition, while the imitation implies the production of dissimilar buildings based on a common set of principles. Put differently, the type can be imitated while the model is copied. Faithful to his modernist convictions, Argan avoided Quatremère's fundamental distinctions between the type and the model, the imitation and the copy. In modernism, after all, typology means the standard production of identical objects in series (*objets-types*), and imitating means copying. Although Argan saw the use of types as necessary for historical knowledge and classification, he definitely believed that the use of types was contrary to architectural invention.[9] Thus as the concept of type was being reintroduced into the architectural discourse in the 1960s it was being simultaneously condemned as a hindrance to invention. Rectifying this confusion was one of the tasks that traditional architects would later undertake.

Milanese architect Aldo Rossi—who also wrote for *Casabella* and was its editor—appropriated Quatremère's concept of type, but his reading differed markedly from that of Argan. Rossi had collaborated with Carlo Aymonino on two studies: *La formazione del concetto di tipologia edilizia* (1965) and the small booklet *La città di Padova* (1966), both of which were based on Muratori's work where urban morphology and building typology were applied as operative methods to understand urban phenomena. But it was in his *L'architettura della città* of 1966 that Rossi contributed his most influential critique and proposed reform of modern architecture. The city, he argued, is a structure of urban artifacts, monuments, a system of streets and squares and their relationship to topography. The city is a product of a certain collectivity that takes meaning from a deep historical rootedness maintained by collective memory, by formal analogy, and embodied in the idea of locus.[10] Buildings may retain their original functions and these functions may change, but buildings are also urban artifacts that were analogical to works of art. Building plans and the layout of cities may change but the idea of locus persists for a long time. Cities and societies transform, yet urban continuity depended, in Rossi's words, on certain permanences that transcended the function of buildings and their changes.[11] Types are such urban artifacts that persist as permanences that are woven into the urban fabric, entertaining a close dialectical relationship with architectural character and with technology. Type, Rossi affirmed, "is the very idea of architecture. It is that which approaches the most the essence of architecture, and despite changes, it is always that which is evident to 'sentiment and reason' as the principle of architecture and the city."[12] His use of the term permanences in the plural serves to recall the rich multiplicity that underlined urban form in the past—a past that still meaningfully enhanced daily life, at least in Italian cities. Rossi's attempts to vigorously reinstate the collective memory embodied in the concepts of type, formal analogy, permanences, and monuments, aimed at opposing the rigidity and symbolic poverty of the prevalent functionalist doctrine. More importantly, reinstating these concepts was intended to be operative or instrumental in the work of architects. In constructing his argument Rossi drew on the works of architects, planners, historians, urban geographers, sociologists, psychologists, and the hauntingly evocative imagery in the capricci of Canaletto and Giorgio di Chirico. Most evocative of all was the deep humanism of Mediterranean cities that Rossi civilly offered as a reform to the current architectural culture in Italy and in Europe.

Under the thematic banner of "Rational Architecture" (with an implied relationship to the *razionalismo* of the 1920s and 1930s), Rossi organized the XVth Triennale of Milano in 1973, exhibiting the work of architects from Europe, Japan, and the United States. For the conference catalogue Ligurian architect Massimo Scolari (b. 1943) wrote his influential polemic *Avanguardia e nuova architettura*. Rejecting functionalism, taking urban morphology and building typology as a basis for eliminating "errors in a process of knowledge centered on historical and formal analysis, on the study of the city as a product,"[13] and striving toward an autonomy of architecture in the face of determining capitalist forces of commercialization, were some of the tenets for a new direction—a proposed refounding of architecture that Scolari termed *la tendenza*. This tendency embodied the convergent ideas of Rossi, Carlo Aymonino, Giorgio Grassi, Ezio Bonfanti, Claudio Baldisseri, Bruno Minardi, Giuseppe Grossi, and others. Scolari also warned against the strictures placed on architecture and criticism by conservative modernists like Bruno Zevi while making overtures to the enigmatic and contagiously pessimistic historian Manfredo Tafuri. It is important to note, however, that notwithstanding his critical stance vis-à-vis modernism Scolari's call for a refounding of architecture was to be unequivocally rooted in the forms of the modern movement.[14] Modernism could be reformed, in the opinion of Scolari and others, by infusing it with humanistic values.

Two years after the XVth Triennale of Milano, Luxembourgian architect Léon Krier (b. 1946) organized a conference and exhibition in London and Barcelona titled *Rational Architecture*, which was followed in 1978 by his editing of an influential book carrying the same title.[15] The architects included Léon Krier, Rob Krier, Aldo Rossi, Massimo Scolari, Carlo Aymonino, Oswald Mathias Ungers, Bernard Huet, Miguel Garay, José Ignacio Linazasoro, François Spoerry, Fernando Montes, Werner Kreis, Ulrich Schaad, Mario Botta, Giorgio Grassi, Antonio Monestiroli, Raffaele Conti, Gianni Braghieri, Şefik Birkiye, Rodrigo Pérez de Arce, Christian de Portzamparc, Taller de Arquitectura, Manuel de Solà-Morales, and others. The expression *Rational Architecture*, Krier clarified, was not intended to revive the *razionalismo* of the 1920s but, rather, the rebuilding of the public realm with a philosophical approach rooted in Enlightenment rationalism, in the order embodied in the European city. To rebuild the city and its architecture rationally required a decisive stand against modernism, against zoning practices, against the forced separation between all the elements that used to constitute a city's life. Urban morphology and building typology needed to become part of urban legislation in order to replace the abstract and mono-functional zones that devastated the city. Not to be limited to formal questions alone, rational architecture must be conceived as part of "an integral vision of society, it has to be part of an urban struggle."[16] The present detrimental building practices that devastated both nature and the city with increasing intensity since the end of the Second World War needed to be resolved through nothing short of a "Reconstruction of the City," affirmed Krier. What *Rational Architecture* clearly demonstrated was that the architects who had been espousing common formal and social beliefs, such as those enunciated above, had by then produced work of sufficient urban and architectural breadth that they could genuinely present a reformative platform. Indeed Krier's very organization of the book into thematic sections pointed to this breadth: the dialectics of urban morphology (the street, the square, the block); the quarter or the city within the city; the integration of new buildings within an existing urban fabric; the role of public buildings; and housing and the urban fabric.

What connected these architects, remarked British architectural historian Anthony Vidler, was the idea of an autonomous architecture. In an essay titled "The Third Typology," in the same book, Vidler observed that if the idea of nature validated classicism, and if the machine validated modernism, the "third typology," by contrast, did not search for a validation outside of architectural form itself, that is, outside of architecture as a sociocultural reality. Rather, the new rational architecture took its legitimation from the typologies of the city, from the accumulated urban wisdom that reached its optimal development in the eighteenth century, from the hierarchical distinction between the public and the private realms, and from urban space being formed by a continuous fabric. The new rationalists rejected the modernist utopian reorganization of the city and society, the fragmentation of the city into zones, and the isolated object-building.

Rational Architecture was introduced by art historian Robert Delevoy, who directed the Institut Supérieur des Arts Décoratifs, housed in the old abbey of La Cambre in Brussels. Founded by Henry van de Velde in 1927, the Institut had maintained a modernist curriculum in architecture and urbanism, painting, sculpture, and industrial design, until parts of the urban curriculum began to be transformed toward the late 1970s under the influence of Belgian architect Maurice Culot (b. 1937), who was professor of urbanism since 1974, with the cooperation of a few professors and assistants including Caroline Mierop and Philippe Lefèbvre. It is significant to note that this group realized the first attempt, in the postwar era, to elaborate a teaching that went in the direction of traditional architecture based on the idea of reconstructing the European city. Many counter-projects were proposed for the reconstruction of historic city centers, for working-class districts, and for reurbanizing industrial areas.[17] The teaching strongly associated urbanism with visions of political justice and anti-industrial resistance, and as such it was at odds with the general curriculum of the Institut as well as the political views of its faculty.[18] In what amounted to an academic coup d'état, in Delevoy's terms, Delevoy, Culot, and their colleagues were removed from their teaching positions. La Cambre was subsequently closed as a school of architecture, although it still operates as an art school.[19] Soon thereafter, the group opened The School of Architecture for the Reconstruction of the City in Brussels, with Delevoy as its president and more than twenty professors and forty students. The school's statutes called for reformative projects and research that were based on a "socialist perspective" with the purpose of "contributing to a global project for a society that is radically different from the aims of an advanced industrialized society; to question the reigning system that organizes the built space and its modes of production; to have recourse to a pedagogical project where reflection, analysis, criticism, and research are stimulated by a profound knowledge of the past while being accompanied with practical work produced in close connection with citizens' associations . . ."[20] Regrettably, the new school did not last, but under the direction of Culot the journal of the *Archives d'architecture moderne* played a leading role in elaborating and disseminating traditional architectural projects and writings until 1990.

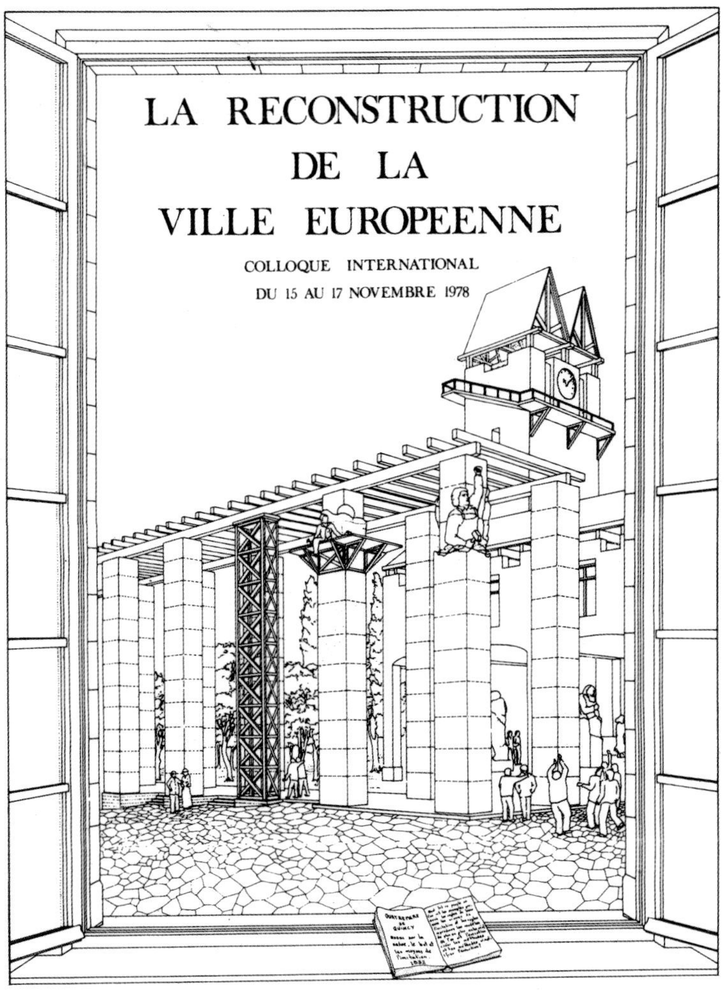

Top: Şefik Birkiye, Gilbert Busieau, Rue Notre-Seigneur and la Place des Brigittines, Marolles, Brussels, 1978

Above: Gilbert Busieau, Şefik Birkiye, Patrice Neyrinck, poster for the international colloquium for the Reconstruction of the European City, Brussels, 1978

The year 1978 also saw two important conferences, and their accompanying polemical declarations, take place in Palermo (April) and in Brussels (November).[21] Both conferences drew attention to the current disarray of cities and architecture caused by: 1) the devastating effects on the city and the countryside by unbridled technological production operating under the guise of progress; 2) the reduction of cities to mono-functional zones that led to absurd and wasteful territorial extensions of the city; 3) the forced exodus of citizens out of the city and their forced daily mobilization back into the city; 4) the destruction of artisanal culture and the transformation of architecture into a consumable production; and 5) the transformation of architecture and the city into the experimental fields for architects' personal idiosyncracies.[22] To remedy these problems, the conferees, who included Krier, Culot, Pierluigi Nicolin, Angelo Villa, Antoine Grumbach, Pierre Laconte, François Loyer, René Schoonbrodt, and Philippe Panerai, presented a set of demands and offered solutions to the European Economic Community. The demands included the rights of citizens to repair the damage that was inflicted on their cities; a recommendation to the E.E.C. to institute commissions that represented local citizens' efforts at reconstructing their cities; and a recommendation for all schools of architecture to orient their teaching toward the reparation of European cities. Reconstructing the city could not happen through the abstractions of zoning but rather through the integrated life of urban quarters where mixed uses occurred in humanly scaled proximities. "Every intervention in a European city must necessarily realize that which was always the city: streets, squares, avenues, blocks, gardens."[23] In criticizing postmodernism directly, the conferees declared that reconstructing the city must transcend the current stylistic experiments that were sometimes proposed as quotes and other times as alternative imageries to dominant modernist forms. The urgency to resolve urban problems could not be obtained by culling architectural forms from history, reducing them to their stylistic dimension alone, and then using them as a form of packaging. The consumer society made for a milieu where architectural culture comes to be consumed as a series of stylistic fragments; and while apologists of postmodernism urged and applauded eclecticism as a sign of creativity, in reality the process was usurped by the vast production of kitsch made inevitable by technological consumerism.

If kitsch, as deception and as a trivialization of artistic culture, rapidly promises and rapidly fails to express any symbolic content, it is because much symbolic thought in architecture and in art had already collapsed. One has but to recall American architect Charles Moore's intention, in his Piazza d'Italia project (1978) for the Italian community in New Orleans, to build a "'Delicatessen Order' that we thought could resemble sausages hanging in a shop window, thus illustrating its transalpine location."[24] Understanding the causes for the collapse of symbolic thought was a necessary step in providing reformatory solutions. Two of the most notable causes were the separation of imitation from invention followed by the confusion of artistic genres. Imitation in art and in architecture provides the intellectual discipline that enables the architect or artist to judiciously select and unify the best aspects of precedents (tradition), while invention seeks to improve the rational choice made from these precedents. With modernism, however, invention became an end in itself. The different facets of the same coin—imitation and invention—now became two identical facets—invention and invention. Artistic and architectural production was now considered to be *all invention*, while imitation collapsed into

Above left: John Russell Pope, Scottish Rite Temple, Washington, D.C., 1915

Above right: Reconstruction of the Temple of Mausolus at Halicarnassus, nineteenth century

Below: Léon Krier, Belvedere, Berlin Tegel, Germany, 1980

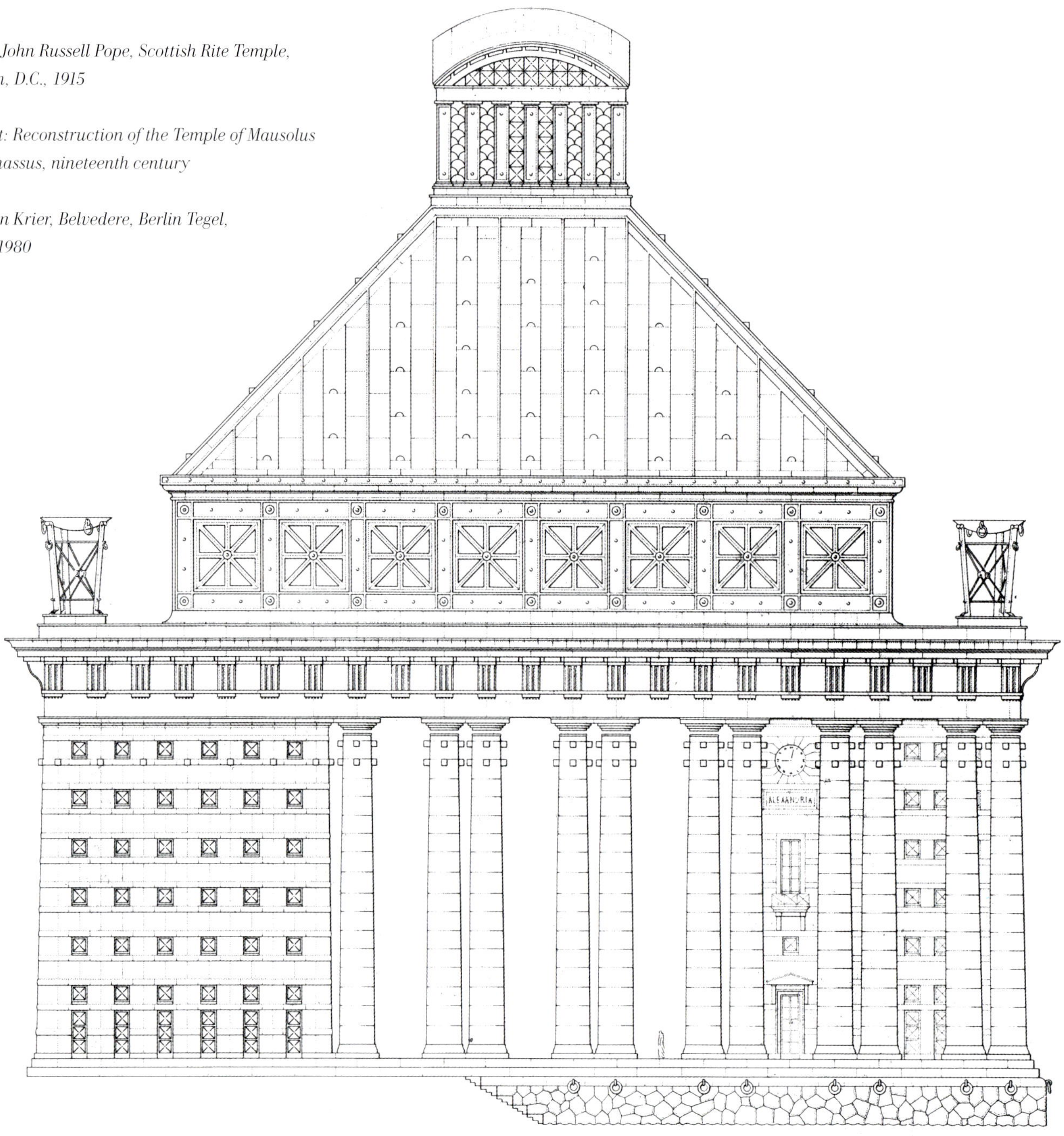

the copy. Imitation and invention thus came to be understood as antagonistic rather than complementary concepts. To be inventive meant that artists and architects were to practice *creatio ex nihilo*, the making of objects out of nothing, following the impulses of their individualistic expressionism. Only, artists and architects do not create in the elementary sense of creation from nothing as their forms are invariably based on older forms—even if they are the inversions or abstractions of previous forms.

Largely eclipsing the difference between the imitation and the copy, the empire of technological means gradually invaded all the arts and exploded the limits between artistic genres. If the considerable *augmentation* of technological means came at the expense of symbolic forms, it is important to note that the extreme *proliferation* of technological means aggressively brushed aside symbolic forms with an intolerant sleight of hand. The natural limits between the arts had been exploded. Thus the distinction between an object of art wrought with artisanal skill and the multiplication of technological processes and products has been blurred. Here we encounter one of the greatest paradoxes of the technological society: on the one hand, the proliferation of objects implies the triumph of the object; on the other, this very proliferation also means the obsolescence of the object—a condition of no sense. Architecture could become painting or sculpture and vice versa. Architects transformed cubist paintings into the plans, sections, and elevations of buildings following the example of modernist prophets such as Le Corbusier. The keyboard of an electric organ produced the sound of drums and cymbals. With the triumph of means any combination of forms becomes possible irrespective of the natural limits or boundaries between the arts, irrespective of artistic genres or established modes of composition. Yet, contrary to prevalent belief, massive technological means did not necessarily facilitate the expansion of artistic freedom, nor the quality of art and architecture. If imitation was separated from invention, invention, in turn, was confused with any technological novelty. If the manifestation of artistic form previously depended on a symbolic thought that instantiated expression and representation through artisanal skill, this manifestation has now been replaced by technical processes and operations and the near elimination of what has hitherto been known as symbolism, or a mythopoeic function. The collapse of symbolic thought was behind the collapse of the imitation into the copy, and for this reason, the collapse of the architectural type into the architectural model. Having lost their distinction, type and model became the technological standard.

To rectify such a collapse required the reclarification and rehabilitation of imitation and invention as inseparable expressions of the human character. With that aim, Léon Krier and Demetri Porphyrios polemically reintroduced into architectural discourse one of the classic texts on imitation: Quatremère de Quincy's *De l'imitation*.[25] Central to Quatremère de Quincy's thought is that imitation produces the resemblance of an object within another object that becomes its image. The imitation reveals one object within another. When applied to architecture, this imitative representation implies a distance between a general type and a particular model, object, or building. It affords the kind of intellectual pleasure that derives precisely from understanding this distance. Imitation is categorically distinguished from the copy that repeats the reality of an object. The copy implies repetition, sameness, counterfeit; it is an object's very double. In *De l'imitation*, Quatremère elaborated on the vital distinction between the imitation and the copy, between "resemblance by means of an image" and "similarity by means of identity."[26] The copy, Quatremère concluded, applied to the mechanical arts, while imitation applied to the fine arts. This prescient distinction, made at a time when industrialization was beginning to displace objects of art, was to obtain in full force with the technological production in series, with the collapse of types into the standard, and finally with the collapse of the imitation into the copy. That is why, having rejected imitation, modernist theorists speak of simulacra. Reintroducing the concept of imitation in art and architecture served to counteract certain theories of representation and their doubtful application to architecture. The resemblance theory, the illusionistic theory, and the semiotic theory applied more readily to other visual arts while carrying a modest degree of relevance to architecture.[27]

Largely as a reaction against the monistic practices of modernism, the postmodern cultural condition encouraged the coexistence of plural artistic forms. Yet, notwithstanding its emancipatory role, postmodernism also engendered a relativism of values that made reasoned judgment difficult precisely because all forms were considered justifiable simply because they were made. Identifying postmodernism as yet another eclecticism, Porphyrios (b. 1949) warned against the risks of "bathing in the pantheistic limbo" of "Modern Eclecticism" in his seminal essay "Classicism Is Not a Style."[28] An increase in eclecticism, or in the proliferation of forms, was not evidence of an increase in inventiveness. Modern traditional architects needed to beware of the consumption of architectural forms, not only on the part of insidious advertising empires that caricaturize architecture, but also on the part of architects who are enthusiastic participants in this consumption. Modern traditional architecture needed to avoid being absorbed into a world that leveled the sense of place and the hierarchical distinctions between private and public architectural expressions. The pluralistic range of modern traditional architecture needed to be founded on the clear distinction between vernacular expression and classical expression, or, as Porphyrios put it, between the *vernacular building craft* and *the art of the classical*. Vernacular building craft refers to the propriety of forms and construction that answer the demands of the private realm, the house, the shop, the office—"an activity that exhibits a catholicity of reason, efficiency, economy, durability and pleasure."[29] The art of the classical designates the propriety of forms and construction that respond to the demands of the public realm, the imitative ennobling or refining of the elements already present in vernacular architecture—an activity of mythopoeic resonance. If piers and beams answer the straightforward demands of building, classical tectonics transcend the contingencies of building in order to produce columnar orders and entablatures. If simple enclosures answered the straightforward demands of shelter, entry, light, and aeration, classical composition articulated the monument, celebrated the gate and the gable, and transformed windows into aedicules. Both the vernacular and the classical operate on two kinds of imitation: 1) imitating the laws of nature (*natura naturans*, e.g. proportion, permanence, gradated forms ranging from heavier to lighter); and 2) imitating that which is most successful in precedents on the urban, architectural, and tectonic scales. Summarizing the broad expressive range from the vernacular to the classical, Porphyrios emphasized that "architecture makes us see the building craft

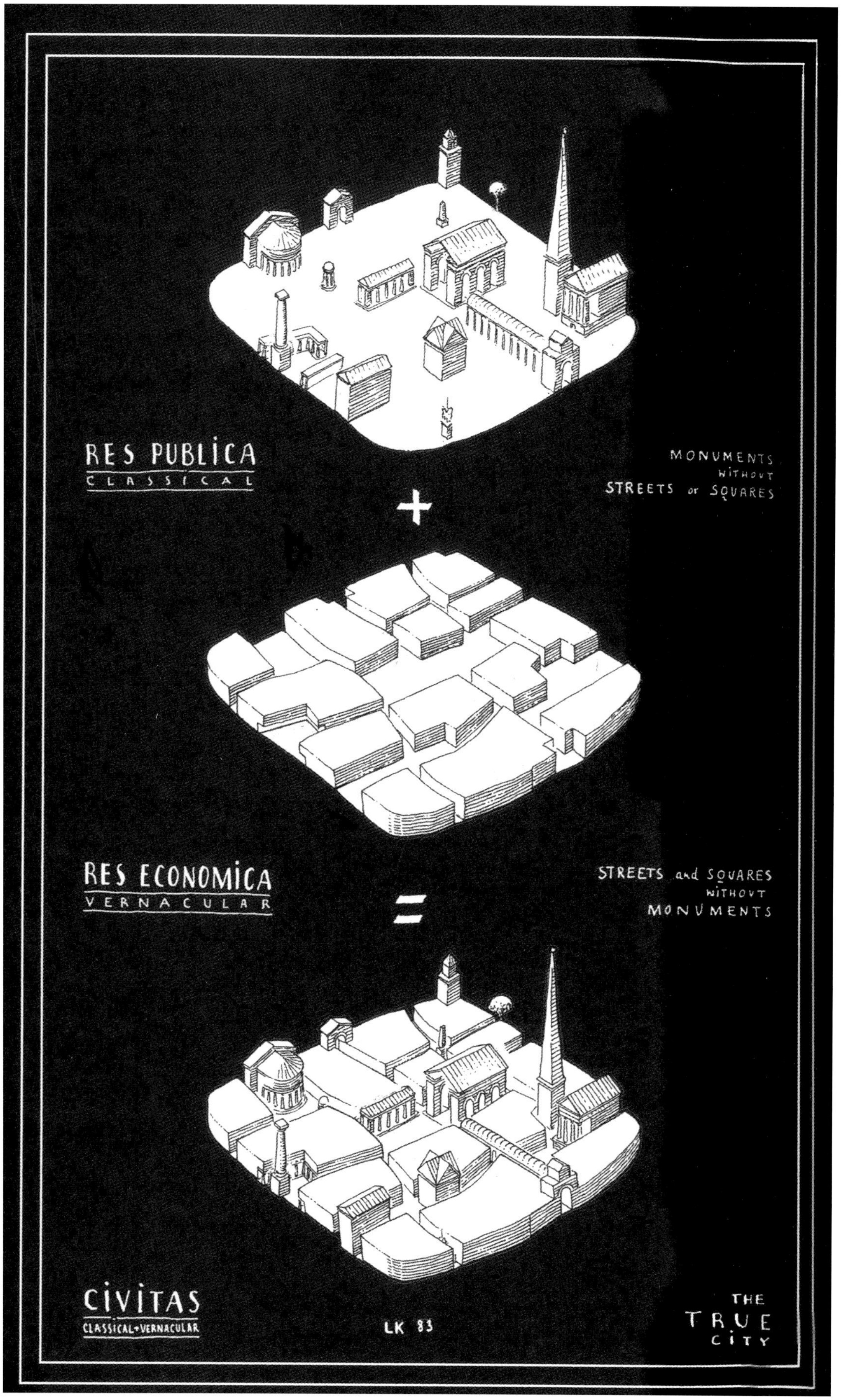

Léon Krier, Civitas, 1983

from which it is born, from which it detaches itself as an art, and to which it alludes."[30]

By the mid- to the late 1980s, the Rationalists had articulated a comprehensive system aimed at reforming two interrelated institutions: practice and the academy. As with all reformatory systems, the justification for proposed improvements is found in the very reasons underlying previous failures; and these failures resided precisely in practice and the academy. First, practice. Against the reduction of the city into mono-functional zones, the Rationalists reasserted the city's composition into quarters, streets, squares, and blocks. Against the segregation of urban components, the Rationalists reaffirmed the dialectical relationship between the public and private realms. Against the destruction of formerly coherent quarters and their replacement by alienating zones of high-rise buildings, they reinstated the value of urban density and the distribution of public and private buildings based on walkability. Against the discounting of buildings into a consumable and pollutive set of technological assemblies, they emphasized enduring building practices and materials (stone, brick, wood). Against the collapse of architecture into technological standards, they reaffirmed architectural typology as an operative basis for practice. The typical is to be categorically distinguished from the typological. Against the symbolic impoverishment of architectural character, they demonstrated the broad range of architectural expression contained between the vernacular and the classical. Against rampant placelessness they asserted the vital importance of regional architectural character.

Second, the academy. Reconstructing the city, for the Rationalists, passed through the reformation of architectural teaching, which in turn implied redressing the prevailing biases of architectural history and theory. Against the prevailing belief that modernism was the exclusive form of modernity possible, the Rationalists proved that tradition, modernity, and the new are perfectly complementary concepts that are always open to evolution and reform. Against the historicist narrative that claimed that history was qualified by one direction that inexorably led to the apotheosis of modernism, the Rationalists underlined the pitfalls of teleological thinking and determinism. Against the prevailing belief that the increase of technological means must necessarily lead to an increase in invention, they showed the contradiction inherent between technological determinism, on the one hand, and individual artistic freedom, on the other. Finally, against their detractors who accused them of repeating preferred architectural forms based on sentimental nostalgia, the Rationalists insisted that their interest in the architecture of the past had little to do with its age-value and much more to do with exemplary architectural qualities that are instrumental in daily practice.

This reconstruction project not only continues to be elaborated but it has since enjoyed breadth and intensification in the profession and in academia now that there are numerous traditional architectural firms throughout the world, two schools of architecture (in the United States), and private institutes dedicated to traditional architecture in several parts of the world.[31] However, if a handful of Rationalists laid much of the theoretical foundations for modern traditional architecture by the early to mid-1980s, the rest of the profession remained mostly hostile with the exception of some postmodernists, some Contextualists, and some New Urbanists who shared certain formal affinities with the Rationalists. One such affinity was an interest in the successful lessons of the past. Here, some commonalities also become reasons for divergences. The Rationalists' understanding of tradition concerns an evolving set of urban and architectural principles and their relation to regional character. The basis of their recuperation of tradition is the use of what has rationally been proven successful in the past and what might rationally prove successful under present exigencies. The Rationalists wish to imitate, not copy, past architectural exemplars. For the Rationalists, traditions change, adapt, migrate, and the possibility for a new tradition to emerge is always present. This approach distinguishes the Rationalists from the Revivalists who practice a traditional architecture with the understanding that tradition has already been fixed and completed. Revivalists delight in their descendance; and their practice in the manner of Vignola, Palladio, the Beaux-Arts, Georgian architecture, Lutyens, or McKim, Mead & White is a perfectly justifiable aesthetic choice in a cultural context that respects intellectual freedom. What the Rationalists reproach the Revivalists for is not their historical connoisseurship or their intimate knowledge of architectural details but, rather, their closeness to their models. The Rationalists criticize modernism for having reduced traditional architectures to their stylistic dimension alone, and then for having dismissed these traditions; but they mildly reproach their Revivalist companions for considering style above all else in architecture. Style is a natural extension of architecture; but there are also types, characters, and tectonics. Conversely, what Revivalists reproach Rationalists for is precisely their distance from the same models, their abstracted tectonic forms, and their search for a symbolic dimension that is purely based in the symbolic logic of tectonics. This is not to suggest that within modern traditional architecture Rationalism and Revivalism should necessarily be considered antagonistic. In a well-furnished architectural world, they can be complementary. If the current architectural (and artistic) condition suffers from much antagonism, much fragmentation, and a severe lack of debate, then the traditionalists, at least, might benefit their profession by lessening the sharp vehemence of their criticism of one another. This touches directly on whether traditional architects consider themselves a movement, or several movements, or no movement at all as we shall see.

Postmodernism

Much has been written about architectural postmodernism as a heterogeneous set of practices that filled the vacuum left by the ideological collapse of modernism—even if building production itself remained mostly modernist. Much more has also been written about the eclectic scenography, the ambiguous allusionism, the ironic and sometimes mocking intentions on the part of postmodern architects to bear repetition here. Notwithstanding the implications of the term postmodernism, many postmodern architects did not wish to completely sever their connection to modernism. Others rejected modernism and worked on connecting with previous traditions. Others still sought to reform modernism by attempting to infuse it with humanist values, with traditional forms, with urban contextualism. American architect Robert A. M. Stern, for example, identified several dualities within postmodernism, which he termed the "doubles of Post-Modern." Most importantly, he distinguished between "1) the schismatic Post-Modernism that argues for a clean break with Western Humanism and a continuity with Modernism and 2) the traditional Post-Modernism that argues for a break with

Modernism and a reintegration with the broader condition of Western Humanism, especially with the Romantic tradition. These seem the only possible categories because they are the only ones that contain 'double' sensibilities of continuity and change which are necessary to sustain generative cycles of creation."[32] While identifying the work of Peter Eisenman as an example of "schismatic Post-Modernism," Stern himself championed what he termed "traditional Post-Modernism" while still holding the view that modernism was definitely part of Western humanism. Of the architects who were called to comment on Arthur Drexler's exhibition *The Architecture of the Ecole des Beaux-Arts* held at the Museum of Modern Art (1975), Stern was one of the few who valued both the work produced in the most important architectural school of the nineteenth century as well as the broad architectural pluralism of that same century. Stern wished to draw a parallel to the present architectural condition where a "post-modernist attitude must be re-established or reaffirmed in words and deeds, the beliefs which were implicit in the vast amount of architecture of the nineteenth century, especially the belief in the power of architecture to achieve symbolic meaning through not only allusions to other moments in architectural history but to historical and contemporary events of the social, political, and cultural nature, are central to the emerging Post-Modern condition."[33]

Of the competing tendencies that qualified postmodernism, four have particular relevance with respect to the imprecise label "postmodern classicism": 1) meaning and the linguistic analogy; 2) pluralism and the uses of tradition (including positions on historical continuity and against historical determinism); 3) architectural composition (including anthropomorphism, geometry, the columnar orders); and 4) urbanism and contextualism. Postmodernists arrived at their uses of traditional forms by traveling on different roads than the ones used by the Rationalists even if both groups drew on similar sources in several architectural traditions while delving into the tradition of the architectural treatise. Since the mid-1960s, as an increasing number of architects gradually began to emphasize humanistic values over functionalism and abstraction, semiotics offered a fertile field of inquiry. Based in part on the work of Ferdinand de Saussure, Charles Sanders Peirce, and others, successive publications were dedicated to applying the methods of linguistic analysis to architecture—a structuralism that considered human expressions as systems of signs connected to meaning.[34] Architects such as Robert Venturi, searched for a kind of architectural symbolism that communicated and carried messages, exemplified especially in buildings along the current American commercial street. In this case, meaning was sought within the framework of a society based on mass consumption, mass media, and mass popular taste. "Each medium," Venturi argues in his second influential book *Learning from Las Vegas* (1972), "has its day, and the rhetorical environmental statements of our time—civic, commercial, or residential—will come from media purely symbolic, perhaps less static and more adaptable to the scale of our environment. The iconography and mixed media of roadside commercial architecture will point the way, if we will look."[35] The great transformation of architectural character by the commercial sign is to a large extent authored by the consumer society, by forces external to architecture and whose influence on architects, Venturi suggests, is a given. His two most quoted expressions—the "decorated shed" and the "duck"—respectively stood for a symbolic content to architecture, which he favored, and for opposing the building that conforms to one single image, itself a sign that stands for certain formal associations given to it by society. Venturi's sharp criticism of the lack of correspondence between "image and substance" in modernism derived from his observation that where modernism wished to achieve symbolism through functionalism, the functional aspect of such elements was frequently found to be deficient, e.g., "glass walls for western exposures" or "the impressions of wooden framework in the concrete of high-labor-cost economies."[36] The kind of symbolism that Venturi championed depended in part on previous forms and associations of meanings with these forms, and he compellingly argues that an "architecture that depends on association in its perception depends on association in its creation."[37] But the symbolic content that Venturi spoke of was only partially linked to the meanings derived from traditional architecture. Symbolic content also derived from a semiotic relation between architectural form and the forms of consumer society with strong links to Pop art. The Gothic church comes to be considered as a building preceded by a facade that announced or advertised the content much like billboard advertising. Semiology considered both the word and the image, the verbal and the visual, as systems of signs containing linguistic and aesthetic functions. Its application to architecture derived in part from theories of perception, and in part from the crisis of meaning pertaining to what historian Joseph Rykwert called a "referential content" in architecture.

Postmodernist architects, and historians, who brought architecture into the semiotic sphere shared the belief that the visual and the verbal are collections of signs. Semiotics became one of the intellectual justifications for postmodernist tendencies. In this sense three of the most notable works on postmodernism in the English-speaking world, Christian Norberg-Schulz's *Intentions in Architecture* (1963), Charles Jencks's *The Language of Post-Modern Architecture* (1977), and *Signs, Symbols and Architecture* (1980), edited by Geoffrey Broadbent, Richard Bunt, and Charles Jencks, were dedicated precisely to the application of semantics, syntax, and metaphor to the modes of architectural expression. Underlying such justificatory analysis of architecture was the assumption that visual systems and verbal systems, or the image and the word, can analogically stand for the same meaning; and at this general level the proposition appears reasonable. A discourse on the value of harmonic proportions in buildings can analogically stand for composing proportionate relationships between the parts of a building. Harmony or proportion can be expressed in many different formal combinations, and meaning arises from the similarities and from the distinctions. This concerns a *semantic analogy* between word and image, or text and building. The *syntactic analogy*, however, presents different problems from the standpoint of makers of verbal and visual forms and from the standpoint of observers of verbal and visual forms. Writers and architects syntactically assemble words and forms according to a system, to a structure, and on that general level, again, the analogy obtains. But the experience of the word in syntax is unlike the experience of the image in visual art. The relationship between a writer and a reader or two people communicating in the same language is not the same as that of the architect and an observer's perception of the architect's building. It is one thing to say that the word can define, explain, represent, and evoke images; it is another to imply a transparent equivalency between the word and the image, or to suggest that they share the same dialectical

Charles Moore, Piazza d'Italia, New Orleans, Louisiana, USA, 1978

Michael Graves, San Juan Capistrano Library, California, USA, 1983

structure. If that were the case, then the verbal and the visual are reducible to each other. They come to be considered as arbitrary yet conventional signs that lead an independent existence until a preconceived meaning is later attached to them. From here derives the larger deduction that not every carrier of message can necessarily be considered a language. The linguistic analogy in architecture is useful precisely if kept on the level of analogy.

American architect Michael Graves (b. 1934) applies the distinction between prose and poetry to architecture in order to distinguish pragmatic building practices from the poetic or symbolic form of architecture. The first he terms internal language, while the second he terms external, that is, an aspect of architecture that is "sensitive to the figurative, associative, and anthropomorphic attitudes in a culture."[38] The poetic language and its anthropomorphic dimension and figurative meaning, he maintains, had been rejected by modernism, which based itself primarily on the machine as "a metaphor." If in the architectures that predate modernism the window mediated between a room and a landscape, and if the window frame in turn related to the body, then in modernism "the window is often continuous with the wall as horizontal banding, or more alarmingly, it becomes the entire surface. The naming of 'window wall' is a prime example of the conflation or confusion of architectural elements. Architectural elements require this distinction, one from another, in much the same way as language requires syntax; without variations among architectural elements, we will loose the anthropomorphic or figurative meaning."[39] While he does not reject modernism in its totality, Graves wishes for architecture to reestablish its link with the mythic and ritualistic dimensions of culture; to realize that purpose, architecture must recover the exemplars of the past: classical antiquity, the Italian Renaissance, the architecture of the Enlightenment.

What in architecture connects to its past or detaches itself from it was the subject of the 1980 Biennale di Venezia, *La presenza del passato* (*The Presence of the Past*). Organized by Paolo Portoghesi, Robert A. M. Stern, Charles Jencks, and others, *The Presence of the Past* grouped the work of over eighty architectural firms from Europe, the United States, South America, and Japan, including Thomas Beeby, John Blatteau, Ricardo Bofill, Maurice Culot, Claudio D'Amato, Jeremy Dixon, Frank Gehry, Michael Graves, Allan Greenberg, Hans Hollein, Léon Krier, Rodolfo Machado, Bruno Minardi, Fernando Montes, Charles Moore, Monta Mozuna, Pierluigi Nicolin, Franco Purini, Aldo Rossi, Massimo Scolari, Jorge Silvetti, Quinlan Terry, Laura Thermes, Thomas Smith, Robert A. M. Stern, Oswald Mathias Ungers, and Venturi, Rauch, & Scott Brown. Portoghesi also asked twenty of the participating architects to build a temporary facade within each of the interior intercolumniations inside the Corderie dell'Arsenale in order to make a *strada novissima*, a new 70-meter-long street. Whereas few of the facades presented a certain conceptual unity, Portoghesi's intent for this architectural eclectic *défilé* was to "return to the street as a constitutive element of the city and which is one of the fundamental terms of post-modern research . . . with special reference to the presence of the past, that is, the role assumed today by reflection on the past as an active basis for design."[40] The conference's effectiveness, and controversy, had less to do with a unified architectural coherence, which it did not intend to have, and more to do with a declaration that a postmodern architectural condition now definitely existed—a condition that was markedly different from the days of the modernist avant-garde.[41] The current condition aimed at establishing a willful distance from established modernism that Portoghesi celebrated as an "end to prohibitionism"—by which he meant the modernist proscription on the uses of traditional forms.

The architectural discipline was beginning to be characterized by an intellectual emancipation breaking away from modernism's bias against the uses of tradition and rejecting the preconceived notion according to which modern architecture was to conform to one single hegemonic expression. This permitted the considerable number of heterogeneous architectural sensibilities to be expressed in a plurality of formal variations and a plurality of meanings derived, in part, from traditional architecture. Yet despite their undeniable usefulness, the traditional tendencies in postmodernism simply affirmed that some form of tradition must be accepted and practiced. But unlike the Rationalist positions, they did not establish a coherent system regarding why traditional architectural forms were to be built, although many members of both groups mutually influenced each other. Nor did the traditional tendencies in postmodernism propose a solid justification for their uses of history. In opposing the ideas that justified modernism (amalgamating the teleological argument in history with the concepts of *zeitgeist* and *weltanschauung*, and with technological determinism), postmodernists declared that not everything in cultural forms is historically determined, nor was modernism the apogee of architectural culture. By attempting to reconnect with humanist values, with the use of traditional forms, by searching for a symbolic dimension within the linguistic analogy, and by distancing themselves from modernism, postmodernists drew attention to the fact that important modifications to the dominant architectural practice and its justifying narrative have become an urgent necessity. The modernist proscriptions on the layered sets of meanings and forms embodied in tradition could no longer be maintained.

Context, Collision, and Collage

In contrast to the modernist fixation on object-buildings, contextualist architects, since the mid-1960s, maintained that urban form and building form must derive from a certain continuity with their direct context. Mindful of the difference between the abstract architectural conceptions of modernism and the demands of site, contextualists recommended that the abstract be transformed when inserted into an urban context. Indeed certain buildings, such as Gunnar Asplund's Royal Chancellery (1922), in Stockholm, were valued precisely because they deferred to preexisting urban conditions. In other words, the site's history and its various contingencies were allowed to shape building form, and vice versa. This was a common point with the Rationalists' dialectic between urban form and architectural types, except that the contextualists did not emphasize typology. The contextualism advocated by historian Colin Rowe and the Cornell studio tried at once to reconcile and alleviate the clash between the traditional city, considered as a solid mass from which figural urban spaces were carved out (exemplified by the figure-ground plan), and the modernist city in the park inhabited by object buildings and surrounded by ubiquitous space.[42] Much of Rowe's work, in fact, never left this dichotomy. But it is important to distinguish between Rowe's contextualism, which was largely an elaboration of urban plans and volumetric studies, and other contemporary views of contextualism that dealt primarily with architectural character and stylistic continuity.

The erosion of the American city presented a particular problem. Its fabric, often a layout of one of several grids, was, by the latter third of the twentieth century, characterized by a pervasive fragmentation. The urban block frequently lacked spatial definition; edges were ill-defined and corners were often missing. This condition was exacerbated by the genuine need for architectural hierarchy, on the one hand, and the nonhierarchical homogeneity of the grid, on the other. Conducting urban investigations of colliding and overlapping grids compelled Colin Rowe and the Cornell studio to develop strategies of collision especially for the large in-between areas that separated two or more fields. At times spaces, and at other times buildings, were given the task of absorbing the accidents and contingencies that emerged from grids in tectonic collision. Urban collision gave way to a strategy of collage, an

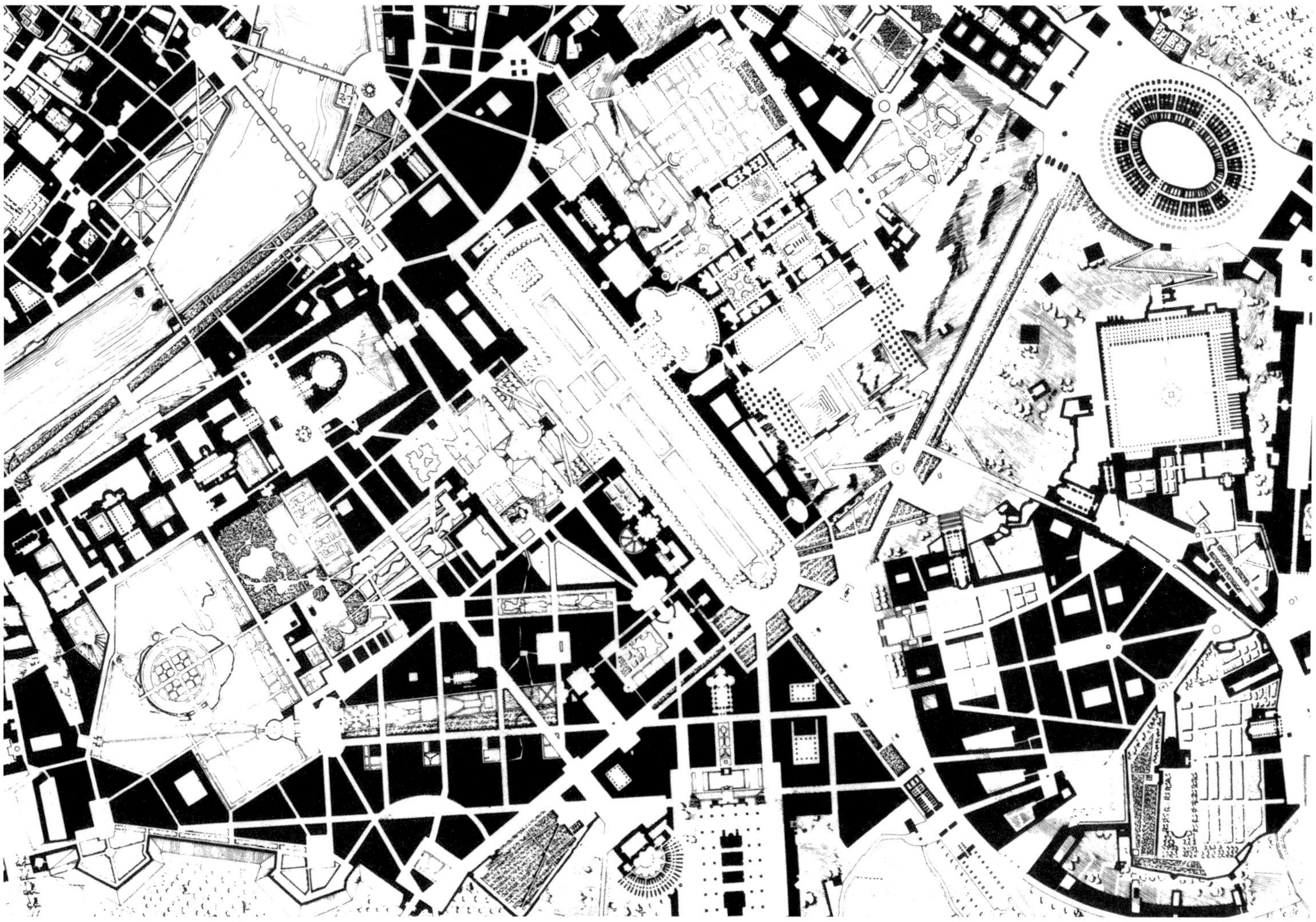

Colin Rowe, Steven Peterson, Judith DiMaio, project for Roma Interrotta, 1978

urban juxtaposition of parts derived from the conception of the city as museum, from Neoclassicism, from the Picturesque, and from Cubist compositional devices. "It is suggested," say Rowe and Fred Koetter, "that a collage approach, an approach in which objects are conscripted or seduced from out of their contexts, is—at the present day—the only way of dealing with the ultimate problems of, either or both, utopia and tradition; and the provenance of architectural objects introduced into the social collage need not be of great consequence. The objects can be aristocratic or they can be 'folkish,' academic or popular. Whether they originate in Pergamum or Dahomey, in Detroit or Dubrovnik, whether their implications are of the twentieth or fifteenth century, is no great matter. Societies assemble themselves according to their own interpretations of absolute reference and traditional value: and, up to a point, collage

Top: Samir Younés, Upper Square, Sidon, The Prince of Wales's Urban Design Task Force for Lebanon, 1997

Above: Léon Krier, Tor Bella Monaca/Aerial View

accommodates both hybrid display and the requirements of self-determination."[43] Rowe and Koetter's collage city was open to using historical exemplars as urban strategies from any period, and as such it was liberated from the strictures of modernism. Borrowing much from the collage method of absorbing fragments incrementally, collage city was less a resolution to a problem than an acknowledgment of the uneasy coexistence between different ways of conceiving cities. Thus, Rowe, and others, attempted a reconciliation between traditional city plans with modernist city plans; and frequently, while the urban plans tended toward the traditional city, the architecture was modernist—an idea that was later absorbed by New Urbanists although with notable transformations. This move was more broadly acceptable to architects who could accept some form of traditional urbanism, at least in plan, while remaining faithful to their modernist formation.

Notwithstanding their transitory state, postmodernism and the context-collision-collage triplicity presented valuable contributions that helped to broaden an architectural consciousness that had become perilously narrow. If modernism was a radical revolution, postmodernism and context-collision-collage were some of the uprisings against this revolution. Architectural historical knowledge could no longer be proscribed, and the new pluralism tolerated many possible uses of tradition. Yet despite the benefits of experimentation with traditional forms, it is important to note that these forms were acquired largely as imagery in the scenographic sense of the word. This explains the lack of tectonic rationality that qualified much in postmodern architecture. To a large extent, postmodernism and the context-collision-collage triplicity remained polemical strategies that did not cohere into a broad system such as the one presented by the Rationalists—a system that embraced the ecological, the urban, the architectural, and the tectonic scales. Architectural polemics justify themselves by tactically opposing other polemics. Architectural systems, however, justify themselves based on a broad embrace of all architectural levels, from city-making to tectonic joinery. For these reasons we emphasized, at the beginning of this essay, the significant distinction between sympathetic antecedents and operative precedents in considering the intellectual lineage of modern traditional architecture. We now turn our attention to three important architectural concepts and their uses.

Tradition, Convention, and the Classical: The Uses and Abuses of Definitions

Movement

Architects and historians use definitions and classifications as parts of their methods of justifying forms, and as ways to include or exclude forms, ideas, and architects. Thus definitions and classifications are directly related to whether traditional architects consider themselves a movement, or several movements, or simply a network of unattached architects who share an abiding interest in tradition as a modern practice. Most traditional architects have thus far avoided referring to themselves as a *movement*. They frequently assert that declaring clusters of architectural forms to be a movement implies, on the one hand, accepting a certain card-carrying orthodoxy and, on the other, classifying dissenting opinions as nonorthodox—as being outside a certain *doxa*. They also declare their aversion to architectural homogeneity and to being wrongfully cast as a homogeneous group. After all, they saw how the severe condemnation of the modern movement was due, in part, to a self-declared avant-garde justifying itself with a self-perpetuating mythology. Traditional architects also know too well that the rivalry that plagues personal and group architectural relationships is frequently accompanied by a kind of excommunication of members of a group. Their concerns extend much further because they are torn between holding a set of principles that they share, on the one hand, and their cherished inveterate individualism on the other. Even if modern traditional architects understand perfectly well that tradition at its very core means a group of minds working jointly on similar ideas and forms, even if they know that architectural making is not a creation from nothing, and even if operative precedents form part and parcel of their intellectual work, they remain the inheritors of the Romantic belief in the architect or artist as a creator who walks in no one's shadow. Their insistence on critical distance makes it difficult for them to embrace a movement even if they hold a considerable number of ideas and forms in common with other traditional architects. This psychological phenomenon is shared by most architects (traditional or otherwise) because few of them separate their architectural convictions from their personae. To put it differently, many architects conflate *to make* with *to be*; and this phenomenon has a direct implication on the formation of movements and their sustainability.

Architects in general, and traditional architects are no exception, jealously guard their costly individualities from one another's judgment, from the multiplicity of competing forms and opinions, as well as their deep rivalries. Understandably, traditional architects also worry about the historian's methods of slicing time into stylistic periods, and the historian's harsh judgment in declaring a cherished movement to be finished. They feel discomfort at being collectively relegated to a periodic slice that erodes their individualities, their uniqueness as makers of form. They enjoy the pluralist cultural context that allows them to practice their intellectual freedom, but at the same time they feel the psychological tensions that result from sharing many commonalities with other traditional architects while insisting on their critical difference with noted furor—and in certain cases this furor reaches pathological levels. Sadly, considerable agreements are frequently sacrificed by giving undue importance to small differences when those small differences serve the vanity of critical difference. The "narcissism of small differences" (Freud's expression) becomes the justification for deep antagonisms among individuals who otherwise have much in common. The peculiar jostling of commonality and critical difference result in a particular kind of rivalry. This rivalry arises once shared ideas and forms clash against the ways in which architects identify their personae with their forms—a *mimetic rivalry*, in the words of French philosopher René Girard.[44]

Definitions

Concepts such as convention, tradition, and the classical are subject to varying definitions and classifications where certain architects are considered traditional, classical, or revivalists. Definitions and classifications are advantageous in so far as they help to identify a wider class of architectural forms as well as distinguishing features for each individual building. Yet in spite of good intentions, definitions and classifications can be abused. They can lead to the *definist fallacy* in which a position is delineated so narrowly and exclusively as to leave no room for alternative definitions and classifications. By contrast, the definist fallacy can delineate a position so broadly as to accept too many alternative definitions and classifications thus rendering useless the very act of defining. An example of the *narrow* definist fallacy is when a building is considered classical only if it includes columnar orders, entablatures, and pediments. An example of the *broad* definist fallacy is when a building is considered traditional simply because it has a sloped roof. But the culture of hypercriticism has frequently undermined good intentions. Conflicts regarding definitions and classifications led to conflicts regarding exceptions to these definitions and classifications. Consequently, the definist fallacy has been a frequent tactic deployed to justify certain architectural identities and exclude others. Yet, although the terms convention, tradition, and classical can be defined too narrowly or too broadly, there are important central meanings about which many will agree.

Convention

Every form of making, of artistic endeavor, depends on conventions that are the conditions of its very existence. Conventions imply an alliance of thought that is collectively elaborated, compared, shared, and transformed; otherwise there could be no conventions (Latin: *con* and *venire*). More than simply inherited common sense, conventions at their best are a *sense-in-common*: the purposeful agreement or consensus-building effort between many minds to elaborate a shared artistic practice. Conventions are poietic and practical, and as such they are the means of imitation and invention. For example, if imitation and invention guide the system and procedures of wood tectonics and their transposition into the system and procedures of stone tectonics, then poietic conventions are used to disseminate the various modes of columnar superposition, of diminution as part of eurythmic adjustments, of the pediment as an idealization of a roof, or the transformation of vernacular buildings into a civic commemorative expression drawing on the cumulative experience of generations in matters of propriety, symmetry, and solidity. Practical conventions are a means to apply and modify precedents to suit the exigencies of present construction with special attention to the details of execution. Conventions converge a broad range of architectural experience, especially the kind of experience that intelligently challenges and improves accepted wisdom. Thus, conventions frequently benefit from license, because while licenses are exceptions to rules, they do not necessarily imply the rejection of rules. Indeed as individual interpretations, some licenses reinforce rules by accepting them as larger collective meanings. Tempered by reason and propriety, license can be useful for invention. Between the modernist rejection of conventions and the traditionalist respect for conventions, we tend to forget that many conventions used to be inventions. Consider, for example, the so-called giant orders adopted by Michelangelo and Palladio and their subsequent inclusion in many buildings as conventional motifs—with varying degrees of success.

Conventions can be taught because they embody the rationality of building that is legitimized by successful experience—but with an important caveat. Too rigid an application of conventions becomes a constriction on inventiveness. Too lax an application of conventions leads from license to caprice, and from caprice to the corruptly uncanny—to the bizarre. When individual taste eclipses collective rationality and becomes the only determining guide, it comes to legitimize individual meanings, the private *doxa*, at the expense of collective meanings or conventions. Indeed, individual interpretation comes to be seen as the logical opposite of conventions—what some architects in the latter half of the twentieth century proudly called the self-referential sign.

Classical

The term classical has had many meanings throughout history and it is given several meanings amongst modern traditional architects as well. Deriving from the Latin *classis* and *classicus*, the term, in Roman antiquity 1) indicated the highest of five social classes according to wealth; 2) it qualified writers whose work was considered to be of the highest or most excellent class as opposed to writers whose prosaic work was metaphorically termed proletarian; 3) it also designated a naval fleet, and the memory of such a designation remains in sites such as the Byzantine complex of Sant'Apollinare in Classe, near Ravenna, a short distance from the ancient port. Ever a synonym to excellence in the visual arts and in literary theory, the concept of the classical in architecture has been used to designate several periods: the Periclean, the Augustan, the Carolingian Renaissance, the Renaissance in many countries since the late fifteenth century, the French seventeenth century, the Baroque period, the so-called Neoclassical period of the late eighteenth and early nineteenth century, and many derivations of these traditions operating well into the twentieth century, as well as the reelaboration of traditional architecture since the 1970s. The term classical has been frequently used as a value judgment associated with maintaining desirable principles such as rationality, harmony, symmetry, propriety, noble simplicity, solidity, enduringness. Most importantly, the terms classical and traditional are entwined with received knowledge and the authority of reason. Put differently, if tradition has authority, it is the authority of reason.

Currently, the term classical is used in three general categories. One application is a historical and cultural category: that which is termed classical designates only the architectures of ancient Greece and Rome as the foundational architectures of Western countries. A second application is slightly broader: that which is termed classical includes the derivatives of Greek and Roman architectures (the Renaissance, the Neoclassical, etc.) in their disseminated movement throughout Europe and North and South America, as well as former colonies around the world. A third application is much more inclusive and cross-cultural in its scope. Indeed, it includes and transcends the first two. It considers the classical as part of a broad range of architectural expression that spans from the private realm to the public realm, respectively designated as the vernacular and the civic. Reasoned comparison between multiple architectural traditions throughout the world reveals that they contain a range of architectural expressions that answer the needs of the most humble private house in the countryside to the most elaborate commemorative public edifice. The composition of architectural elements in modest and private constructions (sills, lintels, rafters, openings) find themselves transformed, refined, ennobled in the composition of buildings that serve the public realm, be it a village or a city. Simple lintels become architraves, ordinary rafters become modillions, windows become aedicules, and a modest porch becomes an impressive arcade. If the constructions of the private realm are termed the vernacular and those of the public realm are termed the classical or civic, then both the vernacular and the classical grow from one another and mutually partake in forming one another with propriety (*decorum*, *convenance*). Put differently, the range between the vernacular and the classical corresponds to the range between construction and architecture—a distinction already present in the Vitruvian text.

The two general categories of architectural expression then, the vernacular and the classical (or the civic), are inseparable. Both partake in forming the sense of place. No city is made of private buildings exclusively nor public edifices exclusively. It is in comparison with private buildings that the civic edifice gains its hierarchical value, its figurative distinction, its proper sovereign monumentality. The city finds its completion in the judicious combination of the private and public realms even if the present condition of many cities betrays a divorce between architectural character and propriety. The architecture of the public realm (e.g., the municipality) is presently in retreat in comparison to the architecture of the private realm (e.g., the office). Powerful private interests use the most ostentatious architectural extravaganzas (e.g., skyscrapers that invert the hierarchy of the public and private realms) served by architects who place their own personal expression over and above the public realm. Building the city, for the foreseeable future, will likely include, at best, fragments of urban order.

By definition, traditional knowledge is rooted in reason and what is deservedly enduring in tradition. Traditional knowledge can ever be renewed, revised, and adapted to best suit present exigencies in view of dwelling enduringly within nature and the city. Blindly repeating a tradition is an affront to reason. Blindly rejecting a tradition is also an affront to reason. The soundness of tradition derives from the soundness of reason. In other words, from the continual reflection, agreement, and disagreement between many free minds contemplating the same concerns and enriched by the wisdom of experience. Continuity is judiciously approved where architectural production has rationally been proven successful, and change is carefully approved where and when there is a rational need to depart from a practice that has failed. Such is the rationality of traditional architecture as a modern practice. Following the hard-earned lessons since the Enlightenment, the practice of tradition stands to benefit from avoiding the belief in an unsurpassable and idealized past, and the belief in an unknown idealized future that will somehow emerge from a technologically determined reality. The use of reason, however, even collective reason, is not a safeguard against error. Consider the urban catastrophes that resulted from the rationality of modernism. Reason can err. It cannot always be vigilant, but it can always be reformed.

Endnotes

1. See the bibliographical chronology at the end of this book.

2. He had adumbrated parts of his method in an essay he published in 1949, "Vita e storia della città." See Emilio De Carli and Elena Scata, eds., *Antologia critica degli scritti di Saverio Muratori, Studi e documenti di architettura*, Studi e documenti di architettura 19 (Florence: Alinea, 1991). Muratori held the chair of Caratteri Distributivi degli Edifici at the Istituto Universitario di Architettura di Venezia, and later the chair of Composizione Architettonica at L'università di Roma.

3. Saverio Muratori, *Studi per una operante storia urbana di Venezia* (Rome: Istituto Poligrafico dello Stato, 1960), 1: 5.

4. Paralleling Muratori's analytical work was the restoration, or rather full restitution, of Bologna's urban fabric, especially the urban blocks, by Pier Luigi Cervellati, who was Assessore al Comune di Bologna from the mid-1960s. See Pier Luigi Cervellati and Roberto Scannavini, *Bologna: politica e metodologia nei centri storici* (Bologna: Il Mulino, 1973).

5. *Studi per una operante storia di Venezia*, 1: 11–40.

6. Traditional architecture continued to be abundantly practiced throughout Italy at the same time as modernist architecture as attested by the work of architects Cesare Bazzani, Armando Brasini, Alberto Calza Bini, Gino Coppedè, Gustavo Giovannoni, Plinio Marconi, Pio Piacentini, Marcello Piacentini, Innocenzo Sabbatini, Federico Frigerio, and many others. See Francesca Romana Stabile, *Regionalismo a Roma, tipi e linguaggi: il caso Garbatella* (Rome: Dedalo, 2001); and Ettore Mazzola, *Contro-storia dell'architettura moderna: Roma 1900–1940* (Florence: Alinea, 2004). The architectures of new towns such as Garbatella and Città-giardino Aniene, albeit within urban plans heavily influenced by the Garden City movement, provided numerous examples of traditional buildings that answered the contemporary needs of housing and the exigencies of economic development.

7. Giulio Carlo Argan, "On the Typology of Architecture," in *Theorizing a New Agenda for Architecture*, ed. Kate Nesbitt, trans. Joseph Rykwert (New York: Princeton Architectural Press, 1996).

8. See A. C. Quatremère de Quincy, "Type," in *The True, The Fictive, and the Real: The Historical Dictionary of Architecture of Quatremère de Quincy*, ed. and trans. Samir Younés (London: Papadakis Publisher, 1999), 254–57.

9. Ibid., 245–46.

10. Aldo Rossi, *L'architettura della città* (Padua: Marcilia, 1966), 20–21.

11. Ibid., 44.

12. Ibid., 27.

13. Michael Hays, ed., *Architectural Theory since 1968* (Cambridge, MA: MIT Press, 1998), 131.

14. Ibid., 132.

15. Léon Krier, ed., *Rational Architecture: The Reconstruction of the European City / Architecture Rationnelle: La Reconstruction de la Ville Européenne* (Brussels: AAM, 1978).

16. Ibid., 35.

17. These projects were exhibited in the *Presenza del Passato* exhibition at the Biennale di Venezia in 1980. See Léon Krier and Maurice Culot, *Contreprojets, Controprogetti, Counterprojects* (Brussels: Archives d'architectures moderne, 1980).

18. On the concept of anti-industrial resistance, see Maurice Culot and Philippe Lefèbvre's essay "The State of Defiance," in *On the Methodology of Architectural History*, ed. Demetri Porphyrios (London: Academy Editions, 1981).

19. See Robert Delevoy, Maurice Culot, and Anne van Loo, *La Cambre, 1928–1978* (Brussels: Archives d'architecture moderne, 1979).

20. "Article 3 des statuts," *Archives d'architecture moderne*, Nº 18, 1980, 85. Author's translation.

21. See André Barey, *La déclaration de Bruxelles* (Brussels: Archives d'architecture moderne, 1980). The contents of both declarations were recast in a single manifesto, "The Only Path for Architecture," jointly written by Culot and Krier for the American journal *Oppositions* 14 (Fall 1978).

22. *Déclaration*, 17–25.

23. Ibid., 23. Author's translation.

24. See Charles Jencks, ed., *Post-Modern Classicism: The New Synthesis* (London: Academy Editions, 1980), 20.

25. A. C. Quatremère de Quincy, *De l'imitation*, (1823), introduction Léon Krier and Demetri Porphyrios (Brussels: Archives d'architecture moderne, 1980).

26. Ibid., 21–28.

27. For a discussion of expression and representation with regard to architecture, see Samir Younés, chapter 7, *The Imperfect City: On Architectural Judgment* (Farnham, UK: Ashgate, 2012).

28. Demetri Porphyrios, "Classicism Is Not a Style," *Architectural Design* 52 (London: Academy Editions, 1982).

29. Ibid., 56.

30. See Demetri Porphyrios "Building and Rational Architecture," *Architectural Design* 54 (London: Academy Editions, 1984), 31.

31. Despite professional and academic hostility, the "first generation" of Modern Traditional Architects were able to teach in a few schools of architecture whose leadership was occasionally sympathetic toward traditional architecture, or at least toward an eclecticism of ideas. An important step was made during Jacquelin Robertson's tenure as dean at the University of Virginia where L. Krier and D. Porphyrios taught traditional architecture from the early to late 1980s, and where Carroll William Westfall, one of the few architectural historians to champion traditional architecture, chaired the division of architectural history until 1998. Krier and Porphyrios continued to teach at Yale University, whose dean, Thomas Beeby, as well as some members of the faculty including architectural historian Vincent Scully and present dean, Robert Stern, were also sympathetic to traditional architecture. A handful of other architects of the same generation were also engaged in teaching courses in traditional architectural composition and analysis such as Rob Krier at the Technical University at Vienna, Jean-François Gabriel at Syracuse University, and Marc Breitman at L'Ecole des Beaux-Arts, Paris-Belleville.

It is also important to note the adumbrations of classical architecture courses and academic programs by the "second generation" of traditional architects. Samir Younés began and taught classical studies and theory classes at The Catholic University of America in 1986–91, and Lucien Steil was academic director of Oregon School of Design in 1988–90. Between 2002 and 2005 a new program in classical and traditional architecture was begun at the Universidade Católica Portguesa in Viseu, with José Cornélio da Silva (director), Lucien Steil, and Alvaro Barbosa.

At present, there are two schools of architecture, much of whose teaching is dedicated to classical and traditional architecture: The University of Notre Dame and the University of Miami. In 1991 the School of Architecture at the University of Notre Dame began a pedagogical program in classical and traditional architecture and urbanism. The program was collectively elaborated by Thomas Gordon Smith (chairman 1991–99), Norman Crowe, Michael Lykoudis (chairman and dean since 2002), Duncan Stroik, Samir Younés (director of Rome Studies 1999–2008), Richard Economakis, Carroll William Westfall (chairman 1999–2002), David Mayernik, Ettore Mazzola, Samantha Salden, Steven Semes (director of Rome studies 2008–11), Aimee Buccellato, Neil Hoyt, Krupali Kruscha, and others. A program in traditional architecture and New Urbanism was collectively elaborated at the University of Miami by Elizabeth Plater-Zyberk (dean 1995–present) with Jorge Hernandez (associate dean 1995–99), Richard John, Oscar Machado, Frank Martinez, Luis and Jorge Trelles, Teófilo Victoria (director of graduate studies 2000–9), Jaime Correa, and others. Also in the mid-1990s the Prince of Wales Institute of Architecture began offering foundation courses, and for a time a graduate course in traditional architecture, with Brian Hanson (as first director), Richard John (as second director), and tutors Robert Adam, Robert Chitham, Dan Cruickshank, Victor Deupi, Liam O'Connor, Hugh Petter, and painters Alexander Creswell and James Hart Dyke, and others. The academic program also included the Visual Islamic and Traditional Arts Programme with Keith Critchlow (director), Khaled Azzam, and others. To this list must be added notable institutes dedicated to classical and traditional architecture: the Institute for Classical Architecture, of New York, with chapters throughout the U.S., the International Network of Traditional Building, Architecture & Urbanism, and, most recently, the Traditional Architecture Group, both in the U.K.

32. Robert Stern, "The Doubles of Post-Modern," in *Robert Stern* (London: Academy Editions, 1980), 65.

33. "Forum: The Beaux-Arts Exhibition," in *Oppositions* 8 (Spring 1977), 171.

34. On architecture and semiotics, see Giovanni Klaus Koenig, *Analisi del linguaggio archittetonico* (Florence: Fiorentina, 1964); Renato de Fusco, *Architettura come mass medium* (Rome: Dedalo, 1967); Umberto Eco, *La struttura assente* (Milan: Bompiani, 1968); Roland Barthes, *Eléments de sémiologie* (Paris: Editions du Seuil, 1968); Maria Luisa Scalvini, *L'architettura come semiotica connotativa* (Milan: Bompiani, 1975); Charles Jencks, *The Language of Post-Modern Architecture* (New York: Rizzoli Publications, 1977); Geoffrey Broadbent, Richard Bunt, Charles Jencks, eds., *Signs, Symbols and Architecture* (Chichester, UK: John Wiley and Sons, 1980).

35. Robert Venturi, Steven Izenour, and Denise Scott Brown, *Learning from Las Vegas* (Cambridge, MA: MIT Press, 1972), 131.

36. Ibid., 137.

37. Ibid., 131.

38. See Michael Graves, "A Case for Figurative Architecture," in *Michael Graves: Buildings and Projects, 1966–1981* (New York: Rizzoli Publications, 1982), 11.

39. Ibid., 11–12.

40. *La presenza del passato* (Venice: Biennale di Venezia, 1980), 38. Author's translation. At the same Biennale M. Culot and L. Krier presented their series of counter-projects.

41. Jean-François Lyotard had just published his important study *La condition post-moderne* (Paris: Minuit, 1979).

42. Conceptions of Contextualism, Collision, and Collage, have been respectively examined in three consecutive chapters in *Collage City*, Colin Rowe and Fred Koetter (Cambridge, MA: MIT Press, 1978), 50–149. For a description of the Cornell architecture studio, see Steven Hurtt, "Conjectures on Urban Form, 1963–82," in *The Cornell Journal of Architecture* 2 (1982): 54–143.

43. *Collage City*, 144–45.

44. See Samir Younés, ed., with René Girard, James Hillman, Léon Krier, and Kent Bloomer, *Architects and Mimetic Rivalry* (London:Papadakis Publisher, 2013).

Projects

Ada Hotel
Türkbükü, Turkey

Ahmet Igdirligil
Bodrum, Turkey

Built in massive loadbearing stone masonry according to local traditions, the Ada Hotel merges harmoniously with its beautiful surroundings, providing comfort as well as a sensitive and articulate massing and building composition. The buildings, built on splendid natural slopes, merge organically with the site, integrating the existing olive trees and creating a fascinating interaction between indoor and outdoor spaces. The hotel complex is a dignified and respectful contribution to a culture of place, enriching and enhancing a sophisticated local building and tourism culture based on the intelligent dialectics of permanence and change and refreshing proposals of invention and adaptation.

Almeria Row
Coral Gables, Florida, USA

DLGV de la Guardia Victoria Architects
Coral Gables, Florida, USA

Almeria Row is a project of ten town houses that introduces a new residential building type to the city of Coral Gables, Florida. The classic town house common in London and New York was adapted to the South Florida climate with the addition of a courtyard inspired by the houses in Seville, Spain. The proportion of the facade, the repetition of the unit, and the proximity of the stoop to the pavement result in a street elevation that is at once familiar and out of the ordinary. The architects have demonstrated both a poetic and professional commitment to the design and production of buildings and towns of exceptional quality informed by history, scholarship, and traditional building arts and craft. Classical architectural principles, vernacular traditions, folklore, and an understanding of contemporary materials and methods of construction contribute to a conception of architecture that is at once reflective and current. As traditionalists, the architects recognize the unique characteristics of individual sites and localities and appreciate the ability of architecture to define a sense of place and to encourage the health of our cities and landscapes. Working with indigenous materials and local craftsmen together with innovative technologies they establish meaningful relationships between buildings and their respective physical and cultural context.

Altanella di Villa Canali
Canali di Reggio Emilia, Italy

Pier Carlo Bontempi
Parma, Italy

The design of a small courtyard composed of two buildings refers to the character and type of local building traditions in the region, which enhance the culture of the rural landscape and the sustainability of the urban context. Villa Canali is situated at the far end of a series of fields facing west with a loggia and porch overlooking the countryside. The *altanella*—a small belvedere on the roof—is its defining characteristic. Built consistently and beautifully in loadbearing masonry with articulated stuccoed walls, and featuring generous and spacious loggias, as well as porches with classically proportioned massing, Villa Canali demonstrates an exceptional harmony between building and landscape. The design refers elegantly to a most delicate dialogue between classical and vernacular principles as well as to creative synergies between the local and the universal.

Amankora
Bhutan

Kerry Hill Architects
Singapore

The design of Amankora, a series of six small lodges located in the Himalayan Kingdom of Bhutan, abstracts the essence of Bhutanese culture, reflecting it in its form, materiality, and spirit. Prominent features of its architecture like its stabilized earth and timber roof structures, building types and forms, proportions and geometries, etc., are all informed by traditional Bhutanese architectural precedents. Amankora offers a relaxed and serene synergy between secular traditions, timeless techniques of construction, forms and materials, and a sophisticated expression of modernity.

The architects have developed a set of standard components that emulate site and program and enhance Bhutanese building traditions. Their roof form adopts the traditional 11-degree pitch common to all Bhutanese buildings. They are built in thick, mass wall construction, using either stone or rammed earth, depending on their location, and, where possible, they are largely devoid of decoration. The buildings are simple, at times monastic, beautifully enhancing an unspoiled landscape.

Artklass Abandoibarra
Bilbao, Spain

Rob Krier, Marc Breitman, Iñaki Aurrekoetxea
Berlin, Germany; Paris, France; Bilbao, Spain

In the context of the revitalization of Bilbao, directed by Cesar Pelli, the construction of the Artklass building has provided the opportunity of developing an exemplary urban project. Built near the Bilbao Fine Arts Museum and in the distant perspective of the Guggenheim Museum, the urban block has been conceived as a traditional lot system reflected in a variety of alternating facades. The volumetrically massive block with 142 high-end apartments is broken up into a total of twenty-three facades emulating the character, rhythm, and urban composition of the historic city. The architecture, with its types, patterns, colors, and textures, is largely inspired by local precedents without merely replicating existing buildings, allowing creative dialogue between localism and globalization. The design has been particularly enriched by the bold articulation of the traditional bay windows, the "*miradores*," and the remarkable dialogue between a classical urban architecture and the thirty-six sculptures by Rob Krier enhancing both the human scale of the city and the resilience of a distinguished humanist culture.

CENTRO COMERCIAL

Arts & Crafts House
Avenel, Kilmacolm, Scotland

Hugh Petter, ADAM Architecture
Winchester, England

This 10-acre site in Kilmacolm, near Glasgow, was lovingly landscaped by its owner in the 1920s. However, the original house was small and incapable of modernization as a family home. The family descendants approached the architect to design six new homes within the gardens, allowing them to control the quality of the buildings and protect the site from over-intensive development. Each of the designs has a unique character and is traditionally inspired, reflecting the established local architecture. The houses disturb as little of the landscape as possible, preserving the unique qualities of this mature landscape setting.

A'Samaliah Island
Abu Dhabi, United Arab Emirates

Fouad Bleibel, Conseco International
Abu Dhabi, United Arab Emirates

This project involved the preparation and implementation of a comprehensive plan to develop A'Samaliah Island into a facility for cultural heritage, education, and tourism. The project has a holistic and humanistic dimension and includes three distinct parts: a sporting zone, a desert/wildlife zone, and a heritage zone, all developed around an underlying theme of environmental conservation and preservation of natural and cultural heritage. The development also includes an entrance harbor/marina and a sailing club and school. The articulate development of a complex architectural program consistently highlighting a sustainable traditional culture completes and enhances an exemplary and ambitious project integrating a full range of architectural scales from landscape to architectural detail. The built environment is treated as an integral part of a comprehensive ecological and cultural endeavor. It establishes both functional-organic and a poetic-artistic relationships in an intelligent, creative, and inspiring synergy of historical memory, traditional know-how, and contemporary expertise.

明
廉
堂

Auditorium Hall, Nanjing University
(former Chapel, University of Nanjing)
Nanjing, China

Zhao Chen
Nanjing, China

This project is one of the most interesting of the didactic, critical, and "philological" restorations, or restorative reconstructions, done by architect Zhao Chen and his collaborators in Nanjing. Their work is based on thorough precedent studies and dedicated typological and architectural analysis and characterized by a consistent implementation of knowledge gained from a historic culture. It is built with correct and appropriate materials and techniques referring to traditional Chinese building crafts and tectonics. It refers also to an excellent design expertise based on time-tested principles of building and place making.

The Bachenheimer Building
Berkeley, California, USA

Kirk E. Peterson & Associates Architects
Oakland, California, USA

The Bachenheimer Building occupies an irregular trapezoidal site, with the composition squaring the corners to create a serene and balanced form. The simple massing is enriched by an eclectic mix of ornament including moldings, recessed arches, colored tile, Gothic panels and eave brackets, and Venetian arcades of redwood. The result is a sort of Berkeley Mediterranean building that is quietly memorable yet clearly congruent with its context. The main tower is off-center on the principal elevation so as to be aligned with the axis of downtown Berkeley's main street. Informed by the beauty, logic, and durability of traditional architecture, and by a deep love for classical and vernacular buildings, the architects expand successfully on an adaptive regional classicism developed throughout the twentieth century at the same time as and in contrast to modernist design.

BUILDING
NEED TRANSIT INFO?
CALL
511
2113

Bahrain Residence
Bahrain

Rafael Manzano Martos
Seville, Spain

Manzano's work spans cultures. Rather than considering traditional Spanish Mudéjar architecture as a defunct historical style of local significance, it emerges as a refreshed and updated design culture perfectly relevant in the modern world. Not only does it successfully operate in its native Spanish context but it proves to be a flexible, adaptive, and extremely efficient design tool in a wide range of geographical settings throughout Europe and the Near and Middle East. It emerged as a style blending Muslim and Christian influences in the twelfth century on the Iberian Peninsula and has remained "contemporary" over many centuries in Spain. The manor house for Faisal Hassan Jawal in Bahrain reflects a precise and almost laconic image of the palace residence as the synthesis of the domestic and the ideal. As stated by Michael Lykoudis, we are in the presence of a "skillful and inspirational ability to render Classical ideals in the local vernacular, blending a multitude of cultural influences into a cohesive whole that respects the past and informs the future."

Bass Library, Yale University
New Haven, Connecticut, USA

HBRA Architects
Chicago, Illinois, USA

Located beneath Cross Campus, one of Yale's most revered spaces, Bass Library is connected to the historic Sterling Memorial Library, whose adjoining lower-level spaces were renovated to achieve a seamless transition between the two buildings. On the green, a new entry pavilion in the Collegiate Gothic style leads to the library below, a matrix of masonry piers, glazed screens, and paneled partitions. A new sky-lit stair adjacent to Sterling's nave provides an alternate route to Bass's vaulted, below-grade spaces. Conceived as an undercroft for Sterling's "cathedral of books," Bass Library employs a transformative architectural vocabulary derived from Yale's masonry walls and ornamental metalwork, suggesting a crypt that supports the Gothic Revival quadrangle above.

The HBRA architects involved in this project were Thomas H. Beeby, Aric Lasher, Gary Ainge, and Michele Silvetti-Schmitt.

Bath House
Gloucestershire, England

Craig Hamilton Architects
Powys, Radnorshire, England

This new bath house is set in the grounds of a historic house in Gloucestershire. The building is designed as a temple and is finished in Bath stone ashlar with a lead roof. The restrained exterior disguises an interior rich in decoration and classical references.

Belhaven
Oregon Coast, USA

Duncan McRoberts Associates
Kirkland, Washington, USA

Belhaven is a small walkable village of thirty-five beach houses on the Oregon coast offering exquisite views of the Pacific Ocean and Cascade Head. The design is conceived as a revival of historical small coastal towns that provided charming destinations away from urban life. Its architecture is simple, well built, and composed in the picturesque manner.
The use of a regional vernacular constructive logic emphasizes a "straightforwardness" of architectural elements with real purpose and function. They are arranged to provide beautiful and harmonious forms complementary to the natural surroundings and thus to honor nature with an abiding sense of place.

Bermuda Village
Coral Gables, Florida, USA

Duany Plater-Zyberk & Company
Miami, Florida, USA

Located on a 3.3-acre site in Coral Gables, Florida, Bermuda Village is a grouping of twenty-two single-family courtyard residences and two duplex compounds arranged in the form of two small city blocks. Rendered in a tropical Bermuda style, the village was created in the spirit of the city's original exotically themed residential "villages" built in the 1920s by developer George Merrick.

Caimitillo House
Panama

Arosemena & Soundy Arquitectos
Panama City, Panama

This residence is the heart of a medley of buildings that the architects began working on in 2007. Like some of the admired Italian villas that influenced its design, it strives to combine pleasure and work: the former in the form of the gardens that surround the residence and provide it with enjoyable views from all its vantage points, and the latter in the form of the organic plantation that edges the garden and that effectively makes this residence a working farm. Throughout the design of the different buildings a strong effort was made to use local materials for their construction and, in various cases, even engaging in their production. The distinctly colored clay that was used for bricks, roof tiles, floor tiles, and road pavers was extracted from the site, giving the buildings a unique and direct connection to the land.

Calabasas Civic Center
Calabasas, California, USA

Robert A. M. Stern Architects
New York, New York, USA

The Calabasas Civic Center gives the city of Calabasas its first opportunity to express in architectural terms the civic ideals of community and environmental stewardship. Calabasas, located in the northwest corner of Los Angeles County, was incorporated in 1992, and city offices and the library have been located in rented space for the past decade. The new Civic Center is situated on a gently sloping site, near arid hills that are a gateway to the Santa Monica Mountains. The arcaded library and city hall are contemporary interpretations of the Mediterranean-style architecture prevalent in Southern California, and are sited informally to create a variety of outdoor spaces, including a grove of olive trees, a civic plaza, and an amphitheater, that together form the public heart of Calabasas.

Caliza Pool
Alys Beach, Florida, USA

Khoury & Vogt Architects
Alys Beach, Florida, USA

Located within a new resort town along the Gulf of Mexico, the Caliza Pool serves as an open-air amenity for its residents and the local community. The splayed site is bounded on the south and west by vehicular streets, on the east by a pedestrian walk, and on the north by a wooded pineland preserve. As the first communal space built within the town, it seeks, by way of its forms and arrangement, to reconnect with the timeless archetype of the Greek *agora*. Rather than gather the program into a single building, it disperses it into a series of *stoas*, each distinct in function and form. These *stoa*, connected by garden walls, contain a raised stone terrace at the center of which lies the main pool, an ellipse of water flush with the paving.

Caliza is the Spanish term for limestone and it is this material, in the form of Dominican shellstone, that thematically links the

many elements of design, from paving to fountains to custom-designed furnishings. The stonework is complemented by a diverse palette of materials, including inlaid beach pebble "rugs," marble mosaic facades, Cuban tile wall panels, and stainless steel curtains. The *stoa* are enlivened by integrally colored plaster walls, while the ensemble as a whole is unified by a continuous veneer of steel-troweled white stucco, which continuously changes color with the light of day. Much as the architecture finds its forms in timeless archetypes, the sustainability of the project is primarily based on principles long established through empirical practice and received wisdom.

Campo Sano Village
Coral Gables, Florida, USA

Duany Plater-Zyberk & Company
Miami, Florida, USA

Continuing in the tradition of Coral Gables's historic villages, Campo Sano Village is a series of town houses in the Dutch Caribbean style. Garage placement creates intimate entry courts, minimizing the impact of parking on the street. Campo Sano Village serves as a model for mid-density housing located along golf courses and other conditions requiring parking access at the front of the lot.

Can Miquel Roig
Santa Gertrudis, Ibiza, Spain

Philippe Rotthier Architecte
Sant Josep, Ibiza, Spain

This house, sheltered for many years in a hillside, was the home of earlier residents on the island. When it was acquired by its new owners it was intact and protected against the elements by an old and resilient corrugated asbestos roof. The architect slowly and carefully deconstructed and reconstructed the roofs, delicately integrated modern technologies and modern comfort, and redesigned the house without damaging the old walls with their layers of lime plaster. Together with the owners he rejuvenated and reinvented the traditional Ibiza *es casament* (the house ensemble together with its commons, gardens, terraces, etc.) reassessing the timeless qualities and perpetual modernity of traditional architecture. Celebrating the harmony, or marriage, of human habitat and nature (*es casament* means both house and wedding) the Can Miquel Roig illustrates the words of Hölderlin: "Full of merit, yet poetically man dwells on this earth."

Cape Dutch House
Coral Gables, Florida, USA

Cúre & Penabad Architects
Miami, Florida, USA

Built in 1926 as a part of the Coral Gables Dutch South African Village and designed by Palm Beach architect Marion Sims Wyeth, the house was restored and perfected by a sensitive refurbishment. Having traveled especially to South Africa to study the original precedents and familiar with its adaptation and variants in Coral Gables, the architects produced an accurate and inspiring paradigm of the fascinating Cape Dutch House. They succeeded in expressing its poetry and rich layers of acclimatized tradition, myth, and memory.

Carnegie Hill Brownstone
New York, New York, USA

Peter Pennoyer Architects
New York, New York, USA

This five-story eighteen-foot-wide town house was originally built as one of a row of four Queen Anne–style houses in 1886. During the first half of the twentieth century, the house was divided into apartments, its emblematic brownstone stoop was removed, and its parlor-floor windows were enlarged and shifted to reflect the reconfigured rooms inside. In restoring it to a single house, the architects reconstructed the entire building down to the party walls, creating an entirely new house set between a restored street facade and a newly designed neo-Federal garden facade with terraces on the setbacks and stairs from the second floor spiraling down to the rear garden. The rooftop addition, contextually designed to recede and to be undetectable from the street, expanded the building to five stories and 5,000 square feet.

Inside the house, what could have been a straightforward renovation of a conventional building type with a predictable plan and section was translated into a moment of inspired design innovation. The focal point of the new interior is a central stair with an atypical double approach from the ground floor ascending to the parlor level. This leads to a vaulted library, inspired by James Wyatt's Heveningham Hall, which runs along the transverse axis and is flanked to the north by a formal sitting room and to the south by a living room with three French doors. With its Art Deco circular grilles, walls of books, glossy ribbing, and series of three arches along the east wall that articulate the stair sequence, the library becomes an unexpected architectural surprise.

The architects collaborated with interior decorator Matthew Patrick Smyth and landscape designer Maureen Hackett, from Hackett Landscape Design.

Casa de Las Lomas
Austin, Texas, USA

Michael G. Imber Architects
San Antonio, Texas, USA

Overlooking the hills of Austin, Texas, this residence captures exemplary views as well as cooling southeast breezes through an open courtyard design. Sustainable building practices were employed through the solid masonry construction and use of modern materials such as aerated autoclave block, allowing for exceptional thermal performance and superior longevity of the structure. The expressive aesthetic of rough-hewn stone, Moorish motifs, and a tiled concrete dome reminiscent of southern Spain feels at home in the Texas landscape. Built into a hillside, the residence is entered on the upper level through a forecourt; here, the parapet of the main entry creates a dramatic silhouette against the Texas sky.

Casa Veloso Matas
Janas, Portugal

Jose Cornelio da Silva
Lisbon, Portugal

Located in a dramatic landscape setting near Sintra, Casa Veloso refers to traditional patterns of Portuguese country houses. Built in load-bearing masonry, it is rendered in lime mortar with the corners highlighted in blue-painted pilasters. The program of the house is articulated in various buildings, composing a compact and complex massing and silhouette integrated harmoniously in a landscape framed by beautiful views of the Sintra hills and the Atlantic Ocean. The layout of the house, both in plan and elevation, refers to "local symmetries" which are consistently used in Portuguese classical architecture and which elegantly reflect the dialogue that has always existed between vernacular and classical architecture in traditional cultures.

Casa Sirena
Las Catalinas, Costa Rica

Arosemena & Soundy Arquitectos
Panama City, Panama

This residence is located on a pedestrian street fronting the Pacific Ocean. It is one of the eight buildings that make up the initial phase of the town of Las Catalinas, which is currently under development in Guanacaste Province, Costa Rica. The founders' aim is to create a largely pedestrian town where the focus of both the urban and architectural designs is the quality of the public realm. All the buildings rise to the edge of their property lines, shaping clearly defined streets and squares while opening up onto private courtyards. The character of the architecture is inspired mainly by Central American precedents from Costa Rica, Nicaragua, Guatemala, Panama, and the Colombian city of Cartagena. Casa Sirena is a four-bedroom L-shaped house that wraps itself around a courtyard. The intention was to create as many quality open spaces in the form of gardens, loggias, balconies, and courts within the compact footprint as would be possible while fulfilling the owner's programmatic needs. To achieve this, all shared spaces such as the living, dining, and kitchen areas are located on the ground floor, where they are privileged with direct openings onto the courtyard. The bedrooms, on the upper floor, open up to balconies and decks which enjoy wonderful views of the courtyard and the ocean.

Casa do Médico
Sines, Portugal

José Baghana & Arquitectos Associados
Lisbon, Portugal

The Casa do Médico de São Rafael facility is located in the town of Sines, on the southern coast of Portugal. The property was acquired by the Portuguese Medical Association in 2005 to create a comfortable retirement and care facility for doctors and includes facilities such as a restaurant and a library. The Casa do Médico also provides assisted residence services to members residing in the vicinity. The project includes the reconstruction of an eighteenth-century manor house in its original form and its articulation with the new buildings. The old Casa de São Rafael farmhouse's external walls and roof were rebuilt and the interior completely renovated, using traditional materials and referring to an appropriate expression of typology and architecture. The other buildings are entirely new, located roughly in the place where the outbuildings of Casa de São Rafael were located, connected by a covered overpass on the first floor, leaving a pedestrian footpath between the two buildings. The Casa do Médico proposes a respectful and elegant compromise between the vernacular traditions of the place and a compelling sense of modernity. The economy of means and the radicalism of simplicity compose a richly suggestive ensemble where historical and contemporary merge harmoniously into a timeless and fascinating synthesis.

New Town of Cayalá
Cayalá, Guatemala

Estudio Urbano, Richard Economakis, Léon Krier
Guatemala; USA; France

The town of Cayalá was master-planned in 2003 by Léon Krier with the Guatemala-based firm of Estudio Urbano, for the local development company Grupo Cayalá. In 2006 and 2008, charrettes were held to fine-tune the master plan and determine the architecture of the buildings, most of which came to be superseded by programmatic, urban, and formal changes. In 2010, supervision of the urban and architectural character of Cayalá was resumed by Estudio Urbano in collaboration with Krier. The design team was composed of Pedro Godoy and María Sánchez of Estudio Urbano, Léon Krier, and Richard Economakis. The designs are being realized by Grupo Cayalá under the supervision of Estudio Urbano team.

Buildings
Phase I: Estudio Urbano—Pedro Godoy and María Sánchez with Léon Krier and Richard Economakis

Phase II (under construction): Estudio Urbano—Pedro Godoy and María Sánchez with Léon Krier and Richard Economakis

The master plan seeks to create a sustainable, mixed-use, pedestrian-oriented environment where buildings reinforce a sense of place and defer to the human scale. Commercial, residential, and other buildings belonging to the private realm are invested with individual character in accordance with their particular site, program, and relationship to the context but contribute at the same time to the making of a congruous urban fabric. The consistency of scale, architectural expression, and materials allows the more elaborated public edifices and monuments to stand out as proper urban set pieces, overturning the established practice of building isolated self-referential object-buildings regardless of use and location. Concern for sustainability has guided many of the decisions made by the design team, for instance the use of natural ventilation and lighting throughout, preference for natural materials over synthetic products, and reduced dependence on the automobile, etc. These approaches are expected to have a positive effect not just on the lifespan of the buildings, but also on the welfare of residents and the economy of Cayalá. With its small urban blocks, three- to four-story building heights, closely knit network of streets and public spaces, and integration of uses, the town facilitates healthy interaction between residents, enhances local and national cultural identity through the use of an architectural language that respects historical precedent, and adapts familiar types for new purposes. Porticos, loggias, and arcades are used liberally in order to take advantage of the site's salubrious climate and spectacular views. Finally, Cayalá establishes a variegated skyline in which towers, domes, and cupolas punctuate the roofscape. These emphasize important buildings and urban nodes, in the manner of traditional towns and cities across Guatemala; the effect contrasts dramatically with the uncompromising uniformity of rooflines in most contemporary developments.

Architectural Expression
The architecture of Cayalá embraces regional Spanish and indigenous traditions, which are employed creatively and adapted to a variety of contemporary building types. These include multistory mixed-use apartments, commercial structures, public buildings such as parking pavilions, cinema complexes, market sheds, and larger civic and sacred edifices. Elevations are typically plastered, with stone trim and moldings. Balconies are either wooden or employ decorative ironwork, and roofs are finished in traditional red tiles. Commercial streets and squares are lined with colonnades that make reference to the characteristic wooden porticos of Spanish plazas in the New World, such as the Parque Central of Antigua Guatemala and the plaza at Santa Fe.

The incorporation of colonnades and terraces along commercial streets is something of an innovation, as in Guatemala and Latin America more generally these features normally occur around squares where public gatherings and celebrations are held. Other nods to local traditions include "figural" windows (octagonal or rosette), stepped tiled cornices, corner bollards, ball finials, consoles, and occasional Mudéjar, or Moorish, details like wall fountains, wooden window lattices, and chamfers. Classical detailing in the more important buildings is derived from Renaissance and Baroque sources of Guatemalan civic architecture. Though treated individually, buildings are designed to work together like good "urban neighbors," the overriding effect being one of variety within unity.

The Krier Tower
Krier's Tower is intended as the principal landmark at Cayalá, marking the southern entrance to the town and the approach from Guatemala City. While its forms make obvious reference to regional details, they are inventively adapted to the vertical proportions and scale of the building. For instance, the projecting stone dados and wooden lattice boxes at the topmost level are derived from familiar Mudéjar forms (the streets of Antigua Guatemala abound with these), as are the deep-projecting eaves. The low-hipped market structure at the base of the building employs the attenuated wooden columns of the traditional Guatemalan portico to form an unusual hypostyle hall. Its long shallow roof is meant to contrast dramatically with the Tower, thereby enhancing its apparent height.

The Athenaeum
The design of the Athenaeum (officially the "Club Cayalá") by Economakis makes reference to a number of regional precedents. For instance, the large steps of the portico evoke the forms of Mayan temples, in particular the complex of Santo Tomás at Chichicastenango, which combines a Pre-Columbian pyramid and Spanish church; the octagonal tower with its crowning lantern alludes to traditional cupolas in the historic city of Antigua Guatemala; the corner windows are derived from a local custom of fenestrating the ends of urban blocks; while the octagonal windows along the east elevation recall the deep-set clerestories along the north facade of the old University of San Carlos Borromeo in Antigua.

The Athenaeum comprises a large ceremonial hall placed on top of street-level shops that open onto a covered arcade/colonnade, lining the west side of the main street. The west elevation of the Athenaeum, which affords dramatic views of Guatemala City and the volcanic landscape beyond, is shaded by a two-story wooden

pergola. Besides their obvious reference to the Mayan temple type, the great steps in front of the Athenaeum at Cayalá are meant to be used as an occasional stage or theatrical cavea for outdoor celebrations.

The Church

The Church of Santa Maria Reina de la Familia by Godoy and Sánchez has been an important feature of the master plan since the first stages of design. Employing classical principles and forms, the building adapts a traditional church type to a sloping site at the northern end of the town. With its Latin cross plan configuration, central dome, barrel-vaulted nave, ancillary chapels, and rows of smaller cupolas over the nave and aisles, Santa Maria Reina will be the first traditional church to be realized in twenty-first-century Guatemala, and the first of this particular type in 203 years. While deferring at the street level to its context of simple three-story plastered volumes, the church stands out as the town's most significant public edifice. This is achieved through its robust massing, rich architectural treatment, profusion of vertical elements, and also by its placement at a point where the most important streets converge, to serve as a visual focus for the entire town.

Public Edifices

The Cayalá master plan provides for three major public edifices, which are a tower by Krier, an Athenaeum (civic hall) by Economakis, and a church by Godoy and Sánchez. Of these buildings, the first to have been completed is the Athenaeum, situated at the center of the town. Phase II will see the realization of the church and tower, which occupy the north and south ends of the master plan.

Central Library
Bam, Iran

Shahriar Yaghini
Bam, Iran

A combination of a cube and three cylinders, this library building has been designed in the manner of the world's largest mud brick structure and a World Heritage monument, the Citadel of Bam. The large cylinder-shaped part of the building accommodates the library's reading hall, while the two smaller cylinders are used for utilities and circulation. The cubic area accommodates the library's seminar hall, offices, and storage spaces. An adjacent orchard was carefully preserved through the construction work and can now be used as an additional outdoor reading area.

Chalet in the Alps
Courchevel, France

Alireza Sagharchi, Stanhope Gate Architecture
London, England

This chalet is one of a few recent new buildings located directly on the slopes of the otherwise fully developed nineteenth-century ski resort town of Courchevel, in the French Alps. The siting of the building is guided by the natural gradient of the mountain. The architecture of the chalet is within the traditional vernacular of Alpine houses and the picturesque tradition of varying volumes with different orientation placed to respond to the panoramic site conditions and long views to and from the building. The pine timberwork on the facade, stone walls, and stone roof have been designed in the local vernacular and executed by craftsmen who have preserved the tradition of building in the mountains for generations.

The interiors of the residence were designed by London decorators Kate Earl and Emily Todhunter, while the exterior details were crafted in collaboration with local architect Jean-Philippe Velghe-Michaux.

CIGARRENMAGAZIN

Charlottenpalais
Berlin-Mitte, Germany

Patzschke & Partner Architekten
Berlin, Germany

This mixed-use building was built in a significant historical location in the center of Berlin when the polemics between the exponents of tradition and those of modernism were at their height. The Charlottenpalais is situated in the Berlin-Mitte, in the center of the ancient Banking Quarter, replacing an unattractive and unsustainable postwar *Plattenbau* in a 35-meter gap between historically registered buildings dating from the Second World War. The new building is characterized by its classically structured facade in stucco and stone, its traditional composition with a rusticated base, a colossal pilaster order, a sophisticated roof area sitting on an articulate and elegant entablature and cornice, its vertical windows and traditionally subdivided window panels, and its exceptional room heights. The facade is composed symmetrically with an enhanced expression of verticality whereas its axiality is stressed by a double-height arched entrance portal.

Churchill Court
Maidenhead, Berkshire, England

John Minshaw Designs
London, England

Churchill Court is a group of elegant garden buildings and follies designed in the eighteenth-century spirit and executed with materials and skills of lasting quality. The site was excavated with a classical pool house built at the lower level, giving the impression that it had been unearthed during an archaeological dig. Double-height doors were used along the entire facade of the building. Three enormous roof lights were supported on Doric columns. The sunken terrace outside the pool house is approached by a flight of steps guarded by hand-carved stone lions and two large urns, the fluting of which twists in different directions so that rainwater can cascade down the steps evenly on each side. The ensemble is completed by a summer house in the form of a miniature Greek temple. The buildings are built in hand-cut Farges stone with elaborate and sharp moldings casting crisp shadows. The stones have mellowed and the copper roofs turned verdigris, weathering naturally into the English landscape.

Citadel Broekpolder
Beverwijk/Heemskerk, Netherlands

K & K Architekten
Berlin, Germany

The development area of Broekpolder is situated between the municipalities of Beverwijk and Heemskerk. Its center, the Citadel, a mixed-use urban quarter, refers typologically to traditional European town building plans and patterns with a strong definition of the urban form and an identifiable center and boundary. The plan is characterized by its row houses, the relatively high density of the scheme, the traditional street and squares, and a rhythmic variation of the block facades. The Citadel is surrounded by a water moat that follows the footprint of an imaginary or mythical fortification. Rather than alluding to any militaristic imagery, this fortress refers to the memory of a clearly legible urban form, the traditional ecological dialectics between countryside and city, and ultimately to poetic images of historic European cities still present in collective memory and imagination.

Cockerill Building
Esch-sur-Alzette, Luxembourg

Mulhern & Steil
Esch-sur-Alzette, Luxembourg

This mixed-use public housing project was built on a large lot in between two unattractive postwar buildings at the edge of the dense inner city overlooking railway tracks and the slopes of a hilly park and forest surroundings. Rather than trying to be literally "contextual," the architects proposed an emulation of context by introducing a dignified and sober classical building. The resulting solution is an urban architecture that is both economical and elegant. The Cockerill Building reflects the highest standards of quality and appropriateness and successfully creates a sense of place and identity. Its composition allies discrete monumentality, symmetry, and proportion to a rigorous definition of the street and urban typology. The Cockerill Building was designed by Mulhern & Steil and built in association with Luxembourg architect Jim Clemes and his firm Architecture & Design.

Coral Gables Museum
Coral Gables, Florida

Jorge L. Hernandez Architect
Coral Gables, Florida, USA

The Coral Gables Museum, a National Register–listed, W.P.A.-commissioned building by Phineas Paist, originally served as the city's police and fire station, jail, and courthouse. The project included the restoration of the masonry, load-bearing coral stone structure, adapting it to the climatic conditions of museum standards while preserving the coral stone surfaces. Both the interior and exterior provided unique challenges. A new wing, the Robert and Marian Fewell Gallery and its adjacent loggia, was added to the north where an existing on-grade parking lot was transformed into a public square. The restoration and new construction were designed for a LEED certification, achieving a Silver rating. The plaza is extensively used for a variety of programs and events.

Cotswold Residence
Stow-on-the-Wold, Gloucestershire, England

Yiangou Architects
Cirencester, Gloucestershire, England

This house built in ashlar from the Guiting quarry is a replacement for a demolished undistinguished 1960s house in the open countryside near Stow-on-the-Wold. It is directly inspired by the strong historicist and Arts and Crafts traditions that define the character of much of the most attractive architecture in the Cotswolds. The front elevation is an asymmetrical composition based on the classic Cotswolds Jacobean E-plan house but becoming progressively more mannered toward the rear, where the elevation is both symmetrical but more informal, using massive oak posts to define the open dining loggia.

New Country House
Hampshire, England

Nigel Anderson, ADAM Architecture
Winchester, Hampshire, England

This new country house replaces an unlisted house on a 930-acre estate in Hampshire and is of a size more appropriate to the location and estate. The historic formal and working yards have been restored and repaired. Alterations have been made to the listed eighteenth-century stable block, cottage, and coach house, along with minor alterations to historic buildings not listed in their own right but considered to be within the grounds of the listed structures. The parkland setting and picturesque landscape have also been restored. The principal elevation with the main entrance door facing the parkland is the most architecturally significant elevation, with a loggia that echoes the entrance of the original house.

Courthouse and Federal Building
Tuscaloosa, Alabama, USA

HBRA Architects
Chicago, Illinois, USA

HBRA Architects' design for the United States Federal Building and Courthouse in Tuscaloosa, Alabama, engages the unique physical and cultural history of the city and the region while incorporating state-of-the-art building systems as well as an Art in Architecture program that reinforces its presence in the cultural landscape. Hierarchical organization of spaces and sequences, modular relationships, and the proportional correlation of interior and exterior elements achieve a singular and enduring expression for the role of the federal government and the courts. Precedents from classical antiquity to the twentieth century were adapted and reconciled so as to provide a timeless building that conveys qualities of permanence and dignity appropriate to its role.

The design team was composed of Thomas H. Beeby, Kirsten Beeby, Craig Brandt, Aric Lasher, Dennis Rupert, William Mahalko, Jerry Wright, Neil Sondgeroth, and Jochen Silvetti-Schmitt. The exterior ornament is by Kent Bloomer, and the interior murals have been crafted by Caleb O'Connor.

UNITED STATES FEDERAL

DING AND COURTHOUSE

Delta Nature Resort
Tulcea, Romania

Alireza Sagharchi, Stanhope Gate Architecture
London, England

The Danube Delta Biosphere Reserve is recognized by Man and the Biosphere (MAB) program of UNESCO and is listed as a wetland of international importance and is included in the Protected Areas category of the *World Heritage List* under the World Cultural and Natural Heritage convention. The delta hosts an amazing range of habitats and life forms in a relatively small area and is a museum of biodiversity. The Delta Nature Resort is also an eco-retreat created for ornithologists and naturalists as well as offering other pursuits and activities such as riding, fishing, and general exploration of wild habitat. The conceptual master plan for the resort was developed by a process of consultation and discussions with the Biosphere Reserve authority with respect to issues such as environment, sustainability, conservation, and protection of natural heritage and use of natural resources. The physical plan of the resort follows the traditional hillside villages found on the Danube Delta as its model for development. The brief has been interpreted and transformed to take the form of a traditional urban settlement where the wood and stone architecture of the buildings follow the same hierarchy of the "public" and "private" elements of the program, each playing the same role as their respective building types in the context of the traditional hillside village.

De Haan, The New Concession
De Haan, Belgium

Maurice Culot, Arcas Paris
Paris, France

The origin of the little Belgian resort town De Haan (Le Coq in French) coincides with the opening of the Hotel Du Coq in 1888. Since 1896 the "Société Anonyme de Coq-sur-Mer" built Anglo-Norman- and English-country-style villas into the dunes. Between the two world wars many villas were built also in Art Deco style. The New Concession project covers an area of 55,000 square meters and follows the local stylistic tradition. It comprises apartments organized along small, gently sloping streets punctuated by agreeable squares. The architectural character of buildings and public spaces encompass a very particular *genius loci* and enhance the typical seaside character of the Belgian coast with its peculiar charm and friendliness.

The Arcas design team was composed of the architects Bart Chielens, Nico Verstuyft, Steve Herzeel, and Hendrik Jacobs.

Dos Flores
Alys Beach, Florida, USA

Khoury & Vogt Architects
Alys Beach, Florida, USA

Dos Flores ("Two Flowers") is the name of the home the architects designed and built for themselves in Alys Beach, a new resort town along the Gulf of Mexico in the Florida panhandle. The house is laid out as an attached courtyard type on a 36-by-80-foot lot. At its heart is the garden court, to which the public rooms of the house open up. While intimate in size, the open court is connected to a series of different outdoor spaces that compose a varied but harmonious sequence of rooms, each with its own character.

The sequence begins at the street, where grandly scaled 11-foot-tall wood gates open up to the *zaguàn*, or vestibule. This open-air hall leads the visitor from the street to the court. Its darker contrast provides a welcome respite from the bright sun-filled street and courtyard beyond as well as leading to the entry

loggia. The gallery, flanking the garden court, is roofed in cedar purlins and a woven cane awning, which filters the light and shades the adjoining interior living rooms. Additional cover is provided by native climbing crossvines planted at each gallery pier.

The gallery leads to the rear garden loggia, an outdoor living room that looks out to the pool and garden court through an Andalusian archway that is mirrored at the entry loggia. Decorative wood panels at its outside wall both light the loggia and cross-ventilate the entire space along its shared axis with the front *zaguàn*.

Drumlin Hall
Dutchess County, New York

Peter Pennoyer Architects
New York, New York, USA

Drumlin Hall, a 7,500-square-foot new classical stone house in Dutchess County, New York, is a modern-day version of a Federal-style villa—a house that revels in perfect proportion, rigorous geometry, and the great flexibility of the classical idiom. Designed to house an important collection of art and furniture, Drumlin Hall illustrates the perfect synthesis of the client's taste, the firm's creative talent, and the contributions of interior decorators, artists, and master craftsmen.

The exterior, faced in warm buff sandstone, with balance, symmetry, and harmonious proportion, bows to the wealth of Regency houses by architects such as Henry Holland, Benjamin Latrobe, Sir John Soane, and S. P. Cockerell. Each of the four principal facades, with its own distinct personality, delights in the possibilities of geometry, graceful proportion, and equilibrium.

The plan of the house revolves around two central axes and contains all of the requisite rooms into a rectangular envelope with windows that express themselves symmetrically on the facades. The interior is characterized by rich and varied classical references and details as well as sophisticated decoration and ornament fusing perfectly art and architecture. The interior decoration for Drumlin Hall has been done by Jayne Design Studio and the landscaping by Ruthie Bontecou of RB Ltd.

Dupont Hall, University of Delaware
Newark, Delaware, USA

Allan Greenberg Architect
Washington, D.C., USA

Dupont Hall, a new research laboratory at the University of Delaware, fills the last site on the Historic Green and completes the master plan designed more than eighty years ago by noted campus architect Charles Klauder. The three-story structure fits seamlessly into the grand tradition of Georgian buildings assembled on the Green over the last century. The new building's character is similar to its neighbors and is respectful of adjacent Wolf Hall, the oldest building on the Green, but injects a lively and distinct personality.

Classical detailing continues from the exterior through to the entrance lobby. The remainder of the interior is designed to emphasize the highly technical aspects of the building's scientific function. Dupont Hall is home to the office of the dean of the College of Engineering, as well as to the Departments of Material Science, Environmental Engineering, and Civil Engineering, and contains state-of-the-art research laboratories and equipment in addition to administrative and faculty office space.

Eau Chien
The Bahamas

DLGV de la Guardia Victoria Architects
Coral Gables, Florida, USA

The traditional role of the porch as a medium between human shelter and the elements (however pleasant these particular elements may be) best explains the enduring presence of classical architecture in the Caribbean. Eau Chien exemplifies this through the prevalent use of the veranda, directly inspired by the rural villas around Rome, in the coastal geography of the Bahamas. As in Palladio, the classical and the vernacular correspond to address questions of climate and culture while contributing to a sense of place.

Ecole Anatole France
Plessis Robinson, France

Breitman-Breitman
Paris, France

A winning entry for an architectural competition, the project for the Ecole Anatole France proposed to restructure a 1930s high school building in the city center and integrate it into a new school project at Plessis Robinson near Paris. Major parts of the existing building were carefully remodeled, crafted, and perfected with many key features maintained and enhanced: the monumental stairs in granite and stone, the auditorium converted into a sports hall, and the large bay window refurbished with new joinery. The new building components were then harmoniously joined to the old components and elegantly articulated around a covered patio. The school has seventeen classrooms, a lecture hall and library, a covered hallway, a restaurant with kitchen, a nursery, and an apartment for the custodian. The sports hall is an independent structure available also for neighborhood activities and local associations. It opens up to the former school yard and its preserved central pavilion.

El Valle Residence
Panama

Arosemena & Soundy Arquitectos
Panama City, Panama

This residence is located in a valley in the central mountain range that extends from South America to North America. The abundance of water and the volcanic soil make this place extremely fertile and abundant in wildlife. The property had a number of large trees, therefore the footprint of the building was kept to an absolute minimum to preserve the greenery. Both architecture and landscape were carefully considered in order to guarantee a minimal site impact and organic integration of buildings and nature. Clay and lime for mortar and paints were used as the basic finishing materials in an attempt to further harmonize the building with its surroundings.

Field Farm Village
Shepton Mallet, Somerset, England

Robert Adam, ADAM Architecture
London, England

Field Farm is a new 42-acre residential district in southwest England built on land owned by the Vagg family and the Prince of Wales's estate, the Duchy of Cornwall. The master plan provides 360 dwellings close to the existing town center, with a housing mix selected to cater to local needs. Other facilities include the original farmhouse and associated parkland, a new school, local shops, a village green, and an old chapel relocated to the site to act as a community building. The design was developed according to traditional principles and has the character of a self-contained village within the larger community of Shepton Mallet.

Fine House
Coral Gables, Florida, USA

Trelles Cabarrocas Architects
Miami, Florida, USA

The Fine House is located in the southern reaches of historic Coral Gables. It is sited on a serene lake surrounded by large lots and a lush subtropical landscape. The beautiful canopy of live oak trees extends all the way to the bay through the Fairchild Tropical Botanic Garden and Matheson Hammock Park, two large and significant preserves that lie immediately east of the neighborhood.

The house's owners desired a Palladian villa adapted for the new millennium. Palladio's villas have long served as models for residences for many considerations: cross-axial plan arrangements and porticoes, threshold space, beauty in the legibility of the building block of virtuous proportions, and the role of the structure in the delivery of a finished work of architecture and those connected to decoration. The site is organized by means of the placement of the house to create new spaces and maintain continuities in the landscape.

Forest of Bere House
Hampshire, England

Julian Bicknell & Associates
Richmond-upon-Thames, England

This new house in Hampshire replaces an earlier farmhouse at the heart of a large agricultural estate on the chalk downlands first occupied by Roman settlers 2,000 years ago. A Roman road passes close to the site, and Roman remains have been found nearby. The new house responds to the landscape and is modeled on a late-seventeenth-century house in the district with elaborately quoined brickwork, high tiled roof, and fine stonework detailing. The outbuildings are treated with the traditional brick-framed flint paneling of this part of England. A walled garden adjoins the family rooms to the west.

The interior combines the rooms of a simple family house with a large hall for the reception of shooting parties and family gatherings. A lantern/observatory and a widow's walk on the roof give spectacular views all around.

Frick Residence
Alpine, New Jersey, USA

Alvin Holm Architects
Philadelphia, Pennsylvania, USA

The Frick Residence in Alpine, New Jersey, was inspired by Mrs. Frick's admiration for the Queen's House in Greenwich by Inigo Jones. Though vastly different in size and scale, the distant relationship can be discerned, at least to the satisfaction of both client and architect, in the two-story entrance facade. The single-story wing of the Frick Residence comprises the formal dining room with an arcade terrace overlooking an extensive apple-tree orchard that slopes down to a small pond with swans. The acorn finials had great appeal to Dr. Frick, who loved trees, and who had rejected the urns the architect first drew as being "gloomy."

The project is characterized by the relationship and dialogue between the architect and his patrons. Ultimately the intimate realms of house, interiors, and garden are engaged with great sensitivity and love of well-crafted details and composition, which respond elegantly to issues of site and context.
Above all the Frick Residence skillfully elaborates on the synergies of classicism and its capacity to articulate the local and the universal, the private and public, the normative and the exceptional.

Gaia Building
Berkeley, California, USA

Kirk Peterson & Associates
Oakland, California, USA

The Gaia Building is a mixed-use structure featuring a live-performance theater on the ground floor. The residential floors above enclose an inner courtyard favoring natural light and ventilation and creating residential comfort and well-being. Extensive multilevel rooftop terraces, inspired by those in Rome, afford views to the nearby wooded hills and through the Golden Gate Bridge to the Pacific Ocean. The basic form of the building refers to warehouse typologies and commercial structures of early-twentieth-century downtown areas in California cities. The ornate crown provides delight to both its residents and to the city and its inhabitants and provides identity and sense of place. Architectural details, such as trellises composed with steel I-beams, are simple adaptations of more formal classical elements.

Georgian House
Northern New Jersey, USA

James Paragano Architect
Morristown, New Jersey, USA

Created in the timeless tradition of classical architecture, this Georgian country estate is designed as a grand symmetrical composition with artfully crafted details. The home is supported by a refined landscape environment encompassing formal terraces and gardens.

Gorinchem Development
Gorinchem, Netherlands

SCALA Architekten
The Hague, Netherlands

This project is located in an industrial area, which became available for housing, in the center of the fortified city of Gorinchem. An urban pattern of streets was added to the formerly closed area, allowing it to connect with the existing urban fabric and to better integrate the fortress-wall with the city. A parking garage was built along the seventeenth-century rampart and topped by a pedestrian boulevard giving access to sixty apartments in different buildings. The smaller streets descending from the boulevard are lined with single-family houses. Traditional stoops are used as a transition between the private and public realms. Both architecture and urbanism of the new development intend to blend into the architectural atmosphere of the city. A great attention and careful consideration was given to accommodate a variety of terraces and balconies oriented to the views on the green rampart and looking out on the river behind.

Granada Court
Pasadena, California, USA

Moule & Polyzoides Architects
Pasadena, California, USA

Courtyard housing is a Southern California walk-up type with attached and stacked dwellings arranged around courtyards and possible direct access to each on all floors without intervening lobbies, elevators, or corridors. In a hybrid courtyard housing form, as in Granada Court, one side of such a building can rise to four stories, with those units being accessed by an elevator and loggia. The extraordinary density of fifty dwellings per acre can then be achieved for a building that enables living around intimate gardens.

The highest purpose for urban housing is accommodating residences that offer both a sense of community and privacy. At Granada Court, privacy is served through a variety of dwelling unit types and sizes. These are flats and town houses located on and above the ground. The outdoor extensions for each unit—yards, porches, belvederes, balconies—are idiosyncratically sized and located to complete the building's aggregate composition. A sense of community is realized through the opportunities to socialize within the building, and also in the strong sense of association that residents feel by living there. The fabric and the figural space of the building promote both.

A tower dominates the corner of the site, and the entire building is massed in parts that are invariably larger than any single dwelling unit, rendering the building place-specific and compatible with the diverse buildings surrounding it. The courtyards are shared, with the fireplace in the entrance courtyard becoming a focus for gatherings. The second courtyard and its fountain become an extension of the community room. A dining terrace and barbecue pit anchor the third courtyard.

Granada Court is built as a wood-frame structure with plaster finish, the simplest and least expensive way to construct in Southern California. It incorporates the most effective regional environmental design strategies: local materials, cross ventilation, natural lighting, high insulation, open-air circulation, ample shading, and direct access to the outdoors.

Halawa House
Agamy, Egypt

Abdel-Wahed El-Wakil
Doha, Qatar

The architect has drawn upon traditional Islamic or Egyptian prototypes for the design of this house. In addition to the courtyard and its fountain, the house has a loggia, a wind catcher, alcoves, masonry benches, and a belvedere. Except for the master mason, plasterer, and carpenter, who were skilled craftsmen, all other labor was by local unskilled Bedouins. The vaults and arches were constructed by the "inclined arch" system without shuttering. The walls and roof are designed to provide good insulation from the harsh climate, sunlight filters through latticed *mashrabiyas*, and the courtyard—which is in shade throughout the day—draws fresh sea air down through the wind catcher. The paving materials also play their part: the marble in the living areas is cool, and the stone used outdoors gives a surface that can be walked on with bare feet even at the height of summer. The design and construction represent a dedicated search for identity characterized by an imaginative handling of traditional vocabulary and the consistent use of traditional methods of construction.

Hanover Lodge
Regent's Park, London

Quinlan & Francis Terry Architects
Dedham, Surrey, England

Built in 1827 in Regent's Park by Decimus Burton, Hanover Lodge was remodeled by Sir Edwin Lutyens in 1910, but much of his work was removed after 1947 when the building became a residence hall for Bedford College. The college left in 1995, the unfortunate 1960s additions were removed, and the Crown Estate offered a lease of the building for use as a private dwelling. In 1996 a wing housing a large reception room with centrally placed bow was added at the rear of the villa. The new building is enhanced by the huge entrance hall with lavishly decorated interiors inspired by Indigo Jones's at Queen's House in Greenwich (1613–35), and by the stone hall at Houghton Hall in Norfolk (1734) by Colen Campbell, James Gibbs, and William Kent. Full-scale freehand drawings by Francis Terry for the decorative stonework and plasterwork introduce a unique vibrancy and sensitivity to forms and associated classical ornament at a remarkable scale.

Hertfordshire Country House
St. Albans, England

Yiangou Architects
Cirencester, Gloucestershire, England

This country house in red brick near St. Albans, outside London, is built on a beautiful open and undeveloped site with stunning views over the countryside. It refers to the English tradition of the gentrified farmhouse with a relatively formal and axial central block housing the more refined living quarters, and informal wings housing the more domestic functions. The details here are spare, almost austere, with the mere suggestion of pilasters in the corners and a simple stone cornice complementing the brickwork. There is a modest Ionic porch to the front elevation and a more striking recessed door with a brick voussoir to the rear. The interior is characterized by an elegant cantilevered stone staircase with cast iron balustrades and a sequence of elegant neoclassical rooms.

Houses
USA

Ferguson & Shamamian Architects
New York, New York, USA

These houses are characterized by the highest standards of classical design. They represent craftsmanship and expertise in historic styles, local vernacular, and regional cultures while remaining refreshingly instructive. The architects excel in the informed and creative use of traditional forms to address unique site conditions and accommodate contemporary needs. The buildings refer to a wide range of precedents that they successfully transcend, achieving highly original arrangements and compositions, and ultimately producing new precedents. These outstanding houses elevate both indoor and outdoor living into an art integrating exquisite interiors and excellent landscaping into a delightful continuum of great integrity and complexity. They encompass a passion for detail, and enhance the use of fine traditional materials and exceptional workmanship, achieving longevity and sustainability.

House on Scottish Island
Scotland

Alireza Sagharchi, Stanhope Gate Architecture
London, England

This country house is located on an extensive estate and is situated within the general context of an officially designated National Scenic Area on the west coast of Scotland. The existing house, a listed monument and a feature of distant views visible from the sea, has fallen into disrepair over the years.
The proposals involve the addition of substantial east and west wings to the house to integrate a pool and a new family wing with the main formal rooms remaining in the original building.

The design philosophy adopted in the refurbishment and extension of the existing house aims to preserve its traditional character. The interiors of the house will be designed by Louise Jones.

The design uses the language of modern traditional architecture and the time-honored character of Scottish vernacular architecture. Use of traditional materials such as scored render and stone are employed in the design of the additions. This ensures harmony with the existing building and emphasizes a relationship that is complementary to the existing house without being a servile copy.

Houses in Toorak
Melbourne, Australia

Christopher Doyle Architects
South Yarra, Victoria, Australia

These houses built in Toorak, a historic suburban area of Melbourne, reaffirm the legacy of the excellent inter-war architecture that characterizes this unique pocket of Melbourne. They attempt to recapture much of the details and qualities that have given historic Melbourne its personality and distinction and to redeem its stirring but short past.

The buildings aim at rediscovering, revalorizing, and emulating the simplicity and modernity of Melbourne's unpretentious structures. They show clearly that their integrity is based upon purpose and proportion. They avoid unnecessary complexity and seek solutions that are firmly based on a simple but elegant tradition. A consistent number of buildings built by the architect in Toorak have achieved a strong local identity and have become respected precedents for new buildings. The projects demonstrate an articulate and rigorous understanding of the classical tradition, local construction, and a respect for enduring structures. It is in no way old-fashioned, sentimental, or nostalgic but rather in tune with a heartfelt desire for authenticity.

Howard Theatre, Downing College, Cambridge University
Cambridge, England

Quinlan & Francis Terry Architects
Dedham, Surrey, England

The new Howard Theatre is the latest addition to the late-Georgian classical campus at Downing College, Cambridge University. It is situated in the newly formed Howard Court, which is made up of two other Quinlan Terry buildings. The new building creates the missing side of the court and in so doing encloses an "outside room" with architectural elements repeated on all three sides. Like the other Terry buildings, it has three stories and a pitched roof. The walls are constructed from Ketton stone with a Doric colonnade.

The architecture of the theater is focused on the auditorium, which is on the first and second floors. It is a small theater with 128 seats downstairs including a single row of chairs down either side beneath a gallery with more seating on the upper floor. The inspiration for the space came from the William Wilkins–designed Theatre Royal in Bury St. Edmunds. Wilkins is of great significance for this project as he not only designed many theaters in East Anglia but he also was the first architect of Downing College.

Immaculate Conception Church
Jefferson, Texas, USA

Curtis & Windham Architects
Houston, Texas, USA

Typical of many Texas communities built in the nineteenth century, the most important civic buildings in the town of Jefferson, Texas, are built of brick and organized around the central town square. The most remarkable architectural feature of the community, however, is its eclectic residential Greek Revival timber structures that are interspersed among the civic and commercial buildings lining the major streets. Adjacent to the gazebo-dominated town square, the new church building is at the physical and spiritual heart of the community and replaces an original structure destroyed by fire. In its reincarnation, the church exterior reflects the simple volumes and ornamentation of the surrounding clapboard houses. Inside, the church is designed to evoke the spirit of the original nineteenth-century structure while respecting the design requirements set forth by Vatican II liturgy.

Pregnant?
Need Help?
665-6020

Indian Creek Residence
Miami, Florida, USA

DLGV de la Guardia Victoria Architects
Coral Gables, Florida, USA

This house is located on Indian Creek in Miami, Florida, with the entrance facing a golf course and with a waterfront facade at the rear. It is a courtyard house designed in the classical style with *coralina* stone columns and cladding. The program includes a two-story residence, gym, playroom, two carriage houses, two pool loggias, and a large lap pool. The project was designed in collaboration with Ernesto Buch Architect, Dominican Republic.

Janzon Residence
Bay Point, Florida, USA

Martinez & Alvarez Architects
Miami, Florida, USA

The Janzon Residence is located in the Bay Point neighborhood of Miami, Florida. The single-family house is designed using vernacular and classical traditions with Scandinavian character and set within and adapted to the site's subtropical environment. The site is an 18,000-square-foot lot fronting a waterway and Biscayne Bay and overlooking Miami Beach. The one- and two-story composition of the house is organized with the ground floor having all of the public rooms including an atrium, loggia, and porches; four bedrooms compose the upper floor.

Kadre Residence
Coral Gables, Florida, USA

Jorge L. Hernandez Architect
Coral Gables, Florida, USA

The Kadre Residence is a contemporary adaptation of the Mediterranean revival traditions of Coral Gables. The rubble coral stone walls and architectural elements are a reference to the use of rubble coral stone throughout the Hammock Lakes neighborhood, once a rock quarry. The character of the two fronts is complementary. The south-facing entry facade is robust and nearly hermetic, and features large planar expanses of white walls that, like canvases, pick up the silhouettes and shadows of a nearby stand of live oaks. The lakefront features expansive areas of glass to connect the principal rooms to the luminous landscape beyond. The house is organized around a large, groin-vaulted double-height living room that serves as the center of social life in the house.

Kensington Palace
London, England

John Simpson & Partners
London, England

A winning entry of an architectural competition, this design proposed a master plan to reorganize Kensington Palace into a major visitor experience and a vibrant community facility. The design incorporates the creation of a new entrance with a new approach from the park that restores the eighteenth-century axis, a new extension providing visitor facilities, a lift inserted into the historic core of the palace to provide level access, and a visitor orientation hub from which the four rationalized narrative routes and exhibition spaces would lead. The master plan encompasses a suite of education rooms, flexible spaces for temporary exhibitions and community use, new conservation rooms and conservation storage for the Royal Court and Ceremonial Dress Collection, and new offices.

La Colina
Punta Cana, Dominican Republic

Ernesto Buch Architect
Punta Cana, Dominican Republic

This house is located at Punta Cana, at the eastern tip of the island of Hispaniola, where the Atlantic Ocean meets the Caribbean Sea. Of the precedents and typologies well suited to this climate the veranda house was of particular interest. Extensive use is made of outdoor living areas such as porches, loggias, and verandas. With tall ceilings and planned for cross ventilation that takes advantage of the prevailing ocean breezes, the house is comfortable without air conditioning most of the time.

Classical architecture was brought to the Caribbean by the European colonizers, with various manifestations of classicism, including Palladianism, adapted to the tropical climate and to local idiosyncrasies. It became an integral part of the building traditions of this region.

This house is built of block walls and a wood frame roof and incorporates a palette of indigenous materials, particularly native stones, such as *coralina*, the beautiful Dominican coral stone. The exterior wall finish is *perrilla*, a stucco material made with crushed *caliza* limestone that requires no painting, its color varying from chalky white to creamy beige depending on the pigment of the stones used.

Lady Margaret Hall
Oxford, England

John Simpson & Partners
London, England

Lady Margaret Hall Master Plan
The master plan, designed as a series of quadrangles evolved in line with the traditional typology of Oxford colleges, unites two isolated buildings built in the 1970s with the historic core of the college. It consolidates the existing buildings with the addition of three new blocks, continuing the character and architecture of LMH begun by Basil Champneys, Reginald Blomfield, and George Gilbert Scott in the early twentieth century and later developed by Raymond Erith in the late 1960s. In the first phase, an L-shaped building provided new undergraduate accommodation as well as a new multipurpose lecture theater–recital room. Phase II incorporates two new buildings in front of the existing austere facade of Erith's unfinished entrance to create a new three-sided quadrangle that gives the college a new public face with appropriate gravitas.

Pipe Partridge Building

The new undergraduate building provides seventy-six individual student rooms that occupy the first and second floors, which can also be used as en suite conference facilities outside term. Continuing the historic layout for women's colleges, each student room is accessible from a central corridor. On the ground floor is a new dining room and adjacent kitchen. Also on the ground floor is a 134-seat lecture theater that incorporates classical interiors and uses acoustic technology so it can be used for lectures, musical performances, and small theatrical productions.

Of solid-masonry construction, the building is constructed using warm red brick in Flemish bond, like that of the other college buildings, with reconstituted stone for dressings that respond to the detailing of the classical buildings by Blomfield, Gilbert Scott, and Erith. The facades are enlivened with cast iron details and a timber colonnade on the northern side. The red-clay-tiled roofs are designed to conceal solar collectors so that an alternative energy source could be incorporated without compromising the design. By placing the solar collectors between the two pitched sides of the roof, the panels are integrated into the design and provide an easy-to-maintain space for services at roof level.

Lakeside Specialist Care Home
Island of Jersey

Robert Adam, ADAM Architecture
Winchester, England

The Lakeside care home is located on an important site on the Rue de la Commune, marking the main approach into St. Peter, Jersey. This location provided an exciting opportunity to create a significant landmark building of the highest quality.
The design is an understated classical building with considered detailing and careful proportioning. The long main facade is set back from the road, allowing for a formal, central approach under the main pediment and porte cochere. Two stepped pavilions flank the entrance, each with central rooftop lanterns and double-height loggias overlooking the surrounding landscape. The simple palette of materials, including lime stucco and cast stone for dressings and moldings, is in keeping with the existing traditional buildings of the area.

La Manzana
Sotogrande, Spain

Rafael Manzano Martos
Sevilla, Spain

La Manzana is a large villa ensemble located in a magnificent setting on the Costa del Sol. The buildings are executed in traditional load-bearing masonry with refined local and natural materials according to the highest standards of traditional craftsmanship. Described as "Andalusian neo-Palladian with a hint of Mudejar," it is simply a beautiful architectural masterwork reflecting the complex layers of Spanish classicism and rich historical Arts and Crafts traditions. La Manzana is both a palace and a city defined by its complex arrangement of buildings and roofs, and their harmonic relationship with the surrounding landscapes and beautifully laid out gardens. The facade of warm ochre tones is characterized by its asymmetries and local symmetries, and enhanced by refined detailing and elegant ornament. La Manzana elegantly displays the rich dialectics between classical and vernacular, imitation and invention, garden and buildings, enclosure and openness, and it articulates a masterful palette of contemporary classicism.

Lehman Residence
Lake Michigan, Illinois, USA

Stuart Cohen & Julie Hacker Architects
Chicago, Illinois, USA

This house is on a suburban site overlooking Lake Michigan. Its design draws from the formal vocabulary of American Arts and Crafts houses and bungalows, and the work of architects such as Greene and Greene. The architects state that it is crucial to work with their clients to understand how they want to live. Referring to the best of traditional architecture, they aim at also providing contemporary living and modern comfort, giving equal importance to interiors and outdoor spaces.

Levin Residence
Coral Gables, Florida, USA

Jorge L. Hernandez Architect
Coral Gables, Florida, USA

The Levin Residence, built in the Hammock Lakes area of Coral Gables, uses striated coral stone and black limestone coursing to create a rustic classicism evocative of the pastoral character of the site. The scale of this large house is mitigated by a picturesque asymmetrical composition featuring elements of local symmetry. The planning strategy and architectural imagery hint at the work of Sir Edwin Lutyens, successfully blending it with local character and atmosphere. Combining seamlessly and organically local and contextual features and references, international references and timeless patterns of classical nature, the Levin Residence achieves a mature and complex excellence, and both a local and universal character.

Mansion House
Mandrogi, Russia

Ivan Kniazev and Alexander Stepanov
Saint Petersburg, Russia

The "Mansion House" is the popular name for this hotel building in the large tourist complex "Verhnie Mandrogi" at the Svir River on the eastern margin of the Leningrad district. This tourist complex was built between 1996 and 2010 in an untamed forest area that is a cruise ship stop on the route to Saint Petersburg. The intent of the project was to showcase the typical image of a Russian village featuring vernacular log cabins (a national building type) mixed with urban middle-class vacation houses and larger-scale mansions. One of the most popular and typical of the latter was defined by Palladian influences popular from the eighteenth century throughout the twentieth century. Mansion House was designed according to these various influences and precedents and has been built completely in traditional timber construction. Its design, composition, and many details are

inspired by the well-known examples of Domenico Gilardi and Joseph Bové and their Moscow Empire–style architecture.

Marbella Houses
Marbella, Spain

Donald Gray
Granada, Andalusia, Spain

The Marbella houses are among many the architect has built in Spain since 1962. Despite their popularity and commercial success, the architect has almost remained mythically anonymous. Though the houses have been designed to blend in with local context, character, material, colors, and style, their contextuality and familiarity reveal an almost heroic indifference to exuberance and the signature of an author. The houses refer to a very thorough knowledge of traditional Spanish architecture and its refined local cultures and craftsmanship. They are comfortably laid out and correctly detailed, and all are beautifully integrated as a part of the city. The houses are organized around streets, alleys, courtyards, and plazas, with the appropriate scale, type, rhythm, and proportions. They seem to have been there forever with a delicate patina and a sense of perpetual freshness and newness. True to themselves and true to their built and cultural context, they refer to both building and dwelling as poetic endeavors.

Apartments in Mayfair
London, England

Alireza Sagharchi, Stanhope Gate Architecture
London, England

This new building comprising eight floors in the traditional context of the Mayfair residential area of London replaces a 1930s apartment block. The original 1750s building that occupied the site was grander in scale and detail than its neighbors, and in early discussion with planning and conservation authorities it was agreed that the replacement building should be of similarly unique character, while continuing the tradition of the neighboring Georgian context.

The pedimented stone facade will be constructed of traditional load-bearing masonry in natural Portland stone. Stone details include a rusticated ground floor, projecting first-floor balcony and corbels, window architraves and entablatures, and an open pediment with acroteria.

The contemporary classical replacement building will be one of the first to be built in Mayfair for decades and will integrate harmoniously with the neighboring Georgian properties while maintaining a unique identity as a modern intervention enhancing the character of the Mayfair conservation area.

McCormick Residence
Martha's Vineyard, Massachusetts, USA

Martinez & Alvarez Architects
Miami, Florida, USA

The Old Baptist Church is located in Edgartown, the island of Martha's Vineyard's first colonial settlement and its county seat since 1642. Edgartown is a harbor town on the island of Martha's Vineyard composed primarily of Greek Revival houses. Wealthy patrons built Edgartown's churches, starting with the First Congregational Church in 1828; this was followed by the Baptist Meeting House in 1839, or "The Old Baptist Church," constructed by the builder/architect Frederick Baylies. The building was poorly converted into a private house in the 1980s, and this redesign involved first restoration and reconstruction of the building's exterior with the goal of bringing back the virtue of the original construction, and second a complete removal/gutting of the compromised interior in order to implement a new residential program without diminishing the intention of the original space in both plan and section.

Mediterranean House
Tallahassee, Florida, USA

Eric Watson, Architect
Tampa, Florida, USA

This new Mediterranean-style house is located on a 5-acre rural site fronting a pond in Tallahassee, Florida. The arrival sequence is a transition from the rough wooded landscape to the more defined formality of the house. Placed on axis with the forecourt but asymmetrically within the entry facade, the Tuscan entry portico marks the arrival to the house. Inside the house, all primary rooms are arranged with access onto porches and terraces to enjoy the view of the rolling lawn and pond beyond. Like the entry forecourt, a level, slightly raised lawn on the garden side of the house transitions the exterior porches and garden areas to the surrounding landscape.

Messila Residence
Kuwait City

Alireza Sagharchi, Stanhope Gate Architecture
London, England

This residence in the Messila district of Kuwait City is designed around the traditional typology of the open courtyard and in a traditional Islamic style where the current trend is for fully enclosed houses that follow a postmodernist architectural language. The traditional typology offers a natural solution to climatic and program challenges of building houses in this region, which often resort to hermetically sealed buildings. Traditional geometry and the golden rectangle, often the organizing element of the patterns and features, are used to compose the facades and volumes as well as the rhythm of the arcuation. The walls are in natural Syrian stone with decorative moldings and motifs highlighting the architectural elements. The intricately laced timber windows and screens give modulation of light and shade to the interior spaces, which were designed by renowned traditional decorator Alidad.

Water reels, pools, and fountains define the inner and semi-open courtyards and connect to the garden beyond.

Montenmedio
Cádiz, Spain

Rafael Manzano Martos
Seville, Spain

Montenmedio serves as a hotel and club for an equestrian and golf resort in Cádiz. Two large existing concrete reservoirs were camouflaged with vegetation and elegantly integrated with their impressive massing and geometry. A classically designed gate was inserted between them to merge them into what looks like an ancient fortress. Organically immersed into the countryside and consistently projecting an architectural presence, Montenmedio is a true landscape monument and architectural landmark as well as a harmonizing, refreshing, and welcoming resort.

Mud House in Mudrapur
Dinajpur District, Bangladesh

Anna Heringer Architecture
Laufen, Germany

These houses were built by Anna Heringer with Khondaker Hasibul Kabir and the assistance of fourteen students and local workers. Seventy-five percent of Bangladeshis live in villages, mostly in loam and bamboo houses, but to improve living standards new houses increasingly use supposedly more durable industrialized materials that are energy intensive and unsuited to the environment. These pilot houses use traditional materials and attempt to boost the local economy and skill base. They increase floor area by adding a story rather than encroaching on land needed for food production. They exploit thermal mass and cross ventilation to save on energy costs and they restore pride in local identity with a modern interpretation of traditional methods.

Museum of São Miguel de Odrinhas, Museum and Arts and Crafts School
Odrinhas, Sintra, Portugal

Alberto Castro Nunes & António Maria Braga
Lisbon, Portugal

Léon Krier, consultant

The Museum of São Miguel de Odrinhas (MASMO), commissioned by the City Council of Sintra, is located near the beautiful royal residence city of Sintra. The purpose of the building was to create a cultural center exhibiting the archaeological collection—mostly Roman but also Neolithic and medieval—in a site that is the oldest Portuguese museum, located around the ruins of a Roman villa. The museum includes a big hall for the Roman epigraphical collection, a gallery for medieval and other archaeological finds, a specialized library, an archaeological working center, an auditorium, and a bookshop. The Arts and Crafts School of Odrinhas, dedicated to teaching traditional building crafts, was built on the other side of the road coming from Sintra. The museum and school ensemble are composed of several buildings that form an urban pattern emulating the character and continuity of the village of Odrinhas.

Netia Piercy House
Bodrum, Turkey

Ahmet Igdirligil
Bodrum, Turkey

The Netia Piercy House is built in traditional load-bearing masonry using local stone. The building is organized comfortably with living room, kitchen, and additional rooms designed as adjacent but separate units. These spaces and rooms are connected to one another in accordance with the natural slope of the land, which allows the roof of one unit to act as the terrace for another; this pattern of organization is very much rooted in the mountain regions of Anatolia. The load-bearing stone walls support a wood joist ceiling. The house is harmonious with a complex topography and a challenging landscape both encompassing the virtue of place, local crafts, and materials. It elaborates poetically on vernacular construction and the delight of classical tectonics.

New Residences
USA

Fairfax & Sammons
New York, New York, USA

New Federal House, Cooperstown, New York
Built on the site of the owner's grandparents' house, this new stone house was intended to become the new family home for generations to come.

Sited on Otsego Lake, the inspiration for James Fenimore Cooper's famed Glimmerglass, it commands a breathtaking view across the water. The house is constructed of load-bearing local stone and is designed in a neo-Federal style, allowing the house to blend in with its neighbors.

The architects have created a fitting centerpiece to a working sporting estate, which restores faith in traditional architectural and rural values. With its hierarchy of spaces and functions, traditional architectural language, and strong relationship to the landscape, Farmlands, as the house is called, is a rural retreat conceived in the manner of earlier country houses, whose owners identified with the land and the pleasures of outdoor pursuits.

New Residence, Southampton, New York
This unique property, a 5-acre site on the north side of Gin Lane, in Southampton, originally had a small unassuming house. The new house, built as a summer retreat, is a seven-bay Georgian shingle house in the Palladian manner, with hyphens and wings, incorporating a double-height front portico in the Ionic order, with painted turned wooden balusters and entablature with painted wood mutules. The front facade has a full terrace in Old Virginia handmade brick and New York bluestone for entertaining guests outside during the summer months, a balcony in the portico, and a widow's walk at the ridge for commanding views of the Atlantic Ocean.

New Georgian Residence, Washington, Connecticut
The ruggedness of the site led the architects to look at Scottish precedent in establishing the character of the design, and much of the detailing and proportioning is inspired by the Scottish Palladian architect William Adam, author of *Vitruvius Scotticus*, and father of the more famous sons. The robust, late-Baroque flourishes found in Adam's work allows the house to establish its presence in the landscape while providing an expression of the owner's own knowledgeable interest in the classical language of architecture. The materials were chosen for their texture: handmade brick with burned headers contrasting with substantially detailed stone cornices, chimney caps, and finials. Inside, paneled rooms have far-reaching views across the landscape.

New Cotswold House
Cotswolds, England

Yiangou Architects
Cirencester, Gloucestershire, England

This large house built of creamy white Hartham Park stone is located in an isolated valley in the Cotswolds. It was built under the special planning circumstances offered by the Planning Policy Guidance (PPG7), a clause stating: "An isolated new house in the countryside may also exceptionally be justified if it is clearly of the highest quality, is truly outstanding in terms of its architecture and landscape design, and would significantly enhance its immediate setting and wider surroundings. Proposals for such development would need to demonstrate that proper account had been taken of the defining characteristics of the local area, including local or regional building traditions and materials." The house is five stories high, both imposing and majestic, but also wonderfully proportioned and sensitive to the scale of the landscape. It referred intelligently to excellent precedents in a select group of tallish early-eighteenth-century houses that exist in the area, while the more intimate and homely appearance is akin to some of the local tall Irish houses. The facade ornamentation, bold window surrounds, keystones, and the shell head porch are elements routinely found in local historic houses. The plan form is compact and consistent, with the stair hall taking up a significant amount of each floor—again an occurrence that exists in many eighteenth-century exemplars and that seemed to offer both compelling and durable qualities of comfort, spaciousness, character, and identity.

Newham
Cornwall

Russell Taylor Architects
London and Cornwall, England

The desire to break with the past, to be different, is creating a placeless landscape and soulless architecture. It has been eroding the patterns and types of traditional English building culture. Newham, on the contrary, achieves a high degree of authenticity and originality, not by fancy or novelty but by using local materials, such as Cornish granite, slate, and rubblestone, and building in a distinctively Cornish tradition with local craftsmen. Like all buildings that are built of good materials and in a sound and careful manner, it has become a harmonious point of focus and an ornament to the landscape. Newham is a classical house designed following principles of composition, proportion, and detailing that have dominated architecture since antiquity. It commands a stunning view over the Fowey River, and is designed both to encompass its site and the building traditions of the place.

Ningboshi Cichengzheng
Cicheng, Ningbo City, China

Zhao Chen
Nanjing, China

This reconstruction of a former government office building in Cicheng, Ningbo City, is not only a rare and beautifully built ensemble but it is also an exemplary and even paradigmatic one. Its excellence of design, composition, and layout as well as the correctness and appropriateness of construction techniques and materials combine the intelligence, knowledge, and craftsmanship that characterize the great classical cultures of the world. It also illustrates convincingly how the harmonious integration of the art and craft, architecture and urbanism, and classical and vernacular expertise of traditional building culture in China can be implemented in a contemporary context and program. The high level of skills and technical competence, and artistic and poetic sensitivity demonstrated in this project is an emergence of a resilient art of building at its highest. The project provides a crucial, viable alternative in a country where one of the world's oldest and most sophisticated urban and architectural cultures is under threat by an acceleration of global industrialism and modernism.

Such projects should be highlighted and rated as the most efficient and operational demonstrations of contemporary genius rather than nostalgic exceptions and diversions. They constitute successful precedents encompassing both identity and modernity. The ultimate aim would be for these to become the didactic models and normative standard for any new construction, both in the context of traditional landscape and urban settings as well as for new developments. With the Ningboshi project, Zhao Chen and his team have achieved a true masterpiece that redefines the theory and methodology of "philological reconstruction" to not only guide the correct and elegant endeavors of historic preservation but to embrace comprehensively all major building tasks of the twenty-first century in a perspective of sustainability and cultural integrity.

思政

North Quad Residential and Academic Complex, University of Michigan
Ann Arbor, Michigan, USA

Robert A. M. Stern Architects
New York, New York, USA

The design for the University of Michigan's North Quad reinforces the Ann Arbor campus's unique architectural and planning traditions with massing and forms based on the very special blend of the collegiate Gothic tradition and the Arts and Crafts that uniquely identify the campus. Working in the first half of the twentieth century, architects Emil Lorch, Pond and Pond, and Albert Kahn designed such buildings as the Union building, the League building, and Lorch Hall, creating a rich tapestry of deep red brick, stone, and slate to shape arcades of flattened arches, grand engaged colonnades, and landmark towers. The architects looked to the tradition of the early-twentieth-century campus as they approached the design of the North Quad in order to shape a new university environment where living, learning, and academic support coexist on a full block anchoring the northwest corner of the main campus.

The North Quad accommodates 360,000 square feet of offices and meeting rooms for various academic departments, classrooms, laboratories, residential suites for students, and dining and social spaces on a tight urban site where the university meets the surrounding town. It rises in a counterclockwise spiral from the dining hall, with its large bay windows overlooking Rackham Green, to the boldly shaped

tower at the southeast plaza, balancing the mass of Rackham Hall. The tower, visible from as far away as the "Diag" (short for Diagonal Green, a large open space in the middle of the campus), terminates the axis of South Thayer Street, thereby constituting a new icon on the university's skyline.

Obrechtstraat
The Hague, Netherlands

Scala Architecten
The Hague, Netherlands

During World War II a long strip of the city of the Hague was cleared as a part of the Atlantic Wall. With its concrete dragon-teeth and bunkers it separated the town from the quarters next to the beach. In the early 1950s a reconstruction plan was carried out by architect Willem Marinus Dudok. This design proposed to reconstruct the strip as a parkway separating the once connected nineteenth-century neighboorhoods. The project was only partially realized, with a small cul-de-sac of the former Obrechtstraat with few remaining terrace houses superficially repaired. Two obvious choices were put forward by Scala Architecten: either finish the Dudok scheme or reconstruct this dead-end street as part of the larger nineteenth-century neighboorhood. The latter option was obviously preferred and promoted by the architects. Two of the existing housing types with porches and small front gardens that previously lined the long street were chosen to rebuild Obrechtstraat.

Ocean Course Clubhouse
Kiawah Island, South Carolina, USA

Robert A. M Stern Architects
New York, New York, USA

This clubhouse for a golf course on Kiawah Island is sensitive to the dramatic but fragile natural landscape of the island's eastern end. The landscape around the clubhouse is elevated significantly not only to maximize views to the eighteenth green and the ocean but also to act as a bridge to reconnect the front nine holes with the back nine. The pro shop and locker rooms face the practice tee and front nine, while hospitality spaces—lounges, dining room, and bar—greet golfers coming from the eighteenth green. The long, low profile of the clubhouse stretches out along the dunes to fit into the rustic character of the link-style course. An entry courtyard welcomes guests, and parking is nestled into the dunes. The picturesque Shingle Style massing of the clubhouse, with deep porches below and dormers above, provides an iconic image for the course.

Our Lady of Guadalupe Seminary and Chapel of Saints Peter and Paul
Denton, Nebraska, USA

Thomas Gordon Smith Architects
South Bend, Indiana, USA

This seminary and chapel are sited upon a hill west of Lincoln, the capital of Nebraska. The complex provides classrooms, a library, a refectory, recreational facilities, and individual rooms for one hundred Catholic seminarians and their teachers, as well as a chapel and cloister. The Priestly Fraternity of St. Peter celebrates and teaches the traditional Latin Mass, now called the Extraordinary Form of the Roman Rite. Such dedication to this tradition determined the most durable construction feasible within their austere budget. The configuration is essentially a monastic layout of institutional and sacred structures around the cloister in emulation of Rome's Romanesque paradigms.

ME ET FACIAM VOS FIERI PISCATORES HOMINUM

Primary School and Community Center
Lijiang Naxizu Zizhixian, China

Li Xiaodong Atelier
Beijing, China

This community service project is in Lijiang, a UNESCO World Heritage Site. It exemplifies the development of regional architecture in the face of rapid globalization and urbanism. Arranged in three blocks, the built form creates two courtyards, one of which is for the community as is the library, giving this low-income society a spiritual center. The architecture looks at the local vernacular from an environmental, social, and conservation perspective using traditional materials and techniques in a contemporary language. Constructed by locals, it has educated them in earthquake-resistant building techniques. It responds to climate and community and as such is sustainable in the broadest sense.

Princess Square
Esher, Surrey, England

Julian Bicknell & Associates
Richmond-upon-Thames, England

Princess Square is a high-density residential development on the outskirts of London. The tightly designed formal square is modeled on eighteenth- and nineteenth-century precedents. It is enclosed on the north side by a new terrace of town houses, to the east by a new range of twelve apartments, and on the south by a group of existing buildings (some dating from the early nineteenth century) now also converted to apartments. The construction is of load-bearing masonry faced with brick and precast stone.

Promontory Point
Texas Hill Country, USA

Michael Imber Architects
San Antonio, Texas, USA

On a site where sprawling suburbia meets the rustic Texas Hill Country, this neighborhood pool house is resolved with a simple but bold structure that provides a public gathering place that so many similar developments lack. The program simply comprised two changing rooms, an office, and mechanical space. A four-part plan was developed and spread a distance apart to increase the scale of the structure to a monumental stature, creating a local landmark. Timber-frame construction provided a straightforward and effective construction technology while expressing classical details such as the Doric columns in the rudimentary vocabulary of local craftsmen.

Punta Cana Church
Punta Cana, Dominican Republic

Ernesto Buch Architect
Punta Cana, Dominican Republic

This new church in Punta Cana was named after Our Lady of Punta Cana and is inspired by a mythical apparition of the Virgin. Commissioned by Grupo Punta Cana, the design was a collaboration of the architect with a firm from Santo Domingo, Zorrilla Baquero. It was also a passionate collaboration with the builder and with a dedicated team—from plasterers to stone masons—who had been working on building houses in the region for the last few years. All donated their labor, not only as a spiritual sacrifice but also out of their dedication to the great tradition of sacred architecture.

Qiblatain Mosque
Medina, Saudi Arabia

Abdel-Wahed El-Wakil
Doha, Qatar

Qiblatain mosque forms an impressive ensemble accommodating up to two thousand worshippers. Beautifully sited in the "Radiant City" of Medina, it is part of a series of large and small mosques built using traditional architectural language and vocabulary as their source of inspiration. The site of the mosque is of particular religious significance, and Muslim worshippers praying at Qiblatain are said to have first changed their direction of prayer from Jerusalem to Mecca in accordance with divine will. The design, ornamentation, and detailing of the new mosque is aimed at enhancing the sense of history and sanctity, and at creating an appropriate atmosphere for meditation for millions of pilgrims visiting the site every year. The major prayer hall adopts rigid orthogonal geometry and symmetry that is accentuated by the use of twin minarets and twin domes. Externally, the architectural vocabulary is inspired by traditional elements and motifs in a deliberate effort to offer an authentic image for a historic site.

Richard Green Gallery
London, England

George Saumarez Smith, ADAM Architecture
Winchester, England

This art gallery at the heart of London's West End provides a new exhibition space for twentieth-century art at Richard Green Gallery. The building has a single-story, bronze-framed shopfront, two principal floors, and a plainer attic story in Portland stone, relating to the existing historic streetscape and retaining the memory of the former buildings on the site. The facade is also an architectural framework for three bas-reliefs by the artist Alexander Stoddart; these pieces illustrate scenes from *The Odyssey*, chosen as an allegory for the development of modern art from 1900 to the present day. The building combines classicism with an appropriate modernity, fitting into this famous street while maintaining a distinct identity.

Sotheby's
33
RICHARD GREEN
33
HUBLOT

De Croissant warme bakker

Riva Development
Amsterdam, Netherlands

Breitman & Breitman
Paris, France

This project is located in a quarter of Amsterdam built in the 1930s and marked by "School of Amsterdam" architecture. The project involved replacing an old garage occupied by the Turkish community and creating a mosque, housing, offices, and shops. The ensemble is organized around a public square that is supposed to receive the mosque in its center.
Shops, offices, and 110 apartments have been completed with the construction of the mosque to follow. The architecture of both private buildings and mosque has been inspired by the neighboring buildings in brick and their characteristic ornaments from the 1930s. The new square overlooks a canal connecting with a main shopping street through a new commercial gallery. The new mosque will be built in brick and timber and refer to Turkish mosque precedents.

River Oaks Boulevard Garden Pavilion
Houston, Texas, USA

Curtis & Windham Architects
Houston, Texas, USA

As part of a comprehensive renovation of this Southern Colonial–style property, an existing freestanding garage was replaced with a new structure that meets the demands of an expanded program while providing architectural focus in the redesigned landscape. Designed by architect Cameron Fairchild in the 1930s, the main house with its double-height colonnade maintains a stately presence on what is the premier boulevard in the Houston neighborhood of River Oaks. Though occupying a similarly modest area as the previous building, the new pavilion structure, in addition to a garage, packs a pool bath, kitchen, and second-floor guest suite into a single compact volume. Positioned on axis with the new pool and ornamented with playful details such as a copper-topped cupola and attic railing, the primary facade of the pavilion plays the role of classical folly in the garden. The secondary pavilion facade, facing the driveway, indicates its more mundane function and is characterized by two garage doors underneath a simple bracketed canopy. Taking its architectural cues from the main house, the double-height Ionic portico overlooking the pool has become the social and visual centerpiece of the new landscape.

Rue St. Vincent
Esch-sur-Alzette, Luxembourg

Lucien Steil
Luxembourg

This urban infill project is located in the historic center of Esch-sur-Alzette in Luxembourg. Intended to introduce social and public housing in the heart of the city, with all its social, cultural, and commercial amenities, the building was inspired by classical town houses and row houses. The design enhances an axial and symmetrical composition, features two balconies on the "piano nobile," and reinforces the structure's center with a cast-stone-framed entrance and an oculus. It is built of load-bearing masonry, with a timber roof structure and natural slate stonework, all completed comfortably within the tight budget of social housing. The painting below, by Rita Wolff, features the Rue St. Vincent project in the form of an architectural *capriccio*.

Saffrin Residence
Lake Forest, Illinois, USA

Thomas N. Rajkovich Architects
Evanston, Illinois, USA

The H-plan configuration of this new residence on Chicago's North Shore creates carefully orchestrated visual and physical connections between the primary interior spaces of the house and a series of outdoor "rooms" of varied landscape and paved treatments. Through the use of salvaged common brick and recycled heavy oak timber for the exterior wall construction, along with the abundance of natural light and ease of natural ventilation provided by the *a la lanterne* plan arrangement, the design demonstrates the fundamental sustainability of traditional building. The classical vocabulary of the house, manifest in the massing, brick detailing, and Tuscan portico, is calibrated to harmonize with the immediate context. This strategy earned the project an award for the sensitivity with which it responded to the historic neighborhood, proving that architecture can inventively participate in the aesthetic

language of its setting without self-conscious abstraction or attention-seeking contrast.

Sales Center
Alys Beach, Florida, USA

Khoury & Vogt Architects
Alys Beach, Florida, USA

Situated along the upper Gulf Coast of Florida, this project is the first building to be completed in a new 160-acre resort town that represents the latest in New Urbanist planning and architecture. It is intended to serve as both an information center and model house for the community, exemplifying the goals and aspirations of the town's founder.

The foremost design challenge was to establish an urban type and architectural syntax that would produce not only interesting houses but a harmonious urbanism for the town as a whole. Toward this end, the attached courtyard, or *patio*, house, as found in the colonial architecture of Latin and South America, was decided upon as a primary architectural type for the residential program.

The architecture of Bermuda is the touchstone for the character of the building and the town. While the tautness and simplicity of its forms supports the making of a calm, relaxed urbanism, it also affords room for sculptural expression, as evidenced in the battered chimney, scalloped gables, and rooftop buttery.

Scheessele House
Charlotte, North Carolina, USA

Grenfell Architecture
Washington, D.C., USA

The design of this house was very much driven by the client's requirement for a true and authentic Palladian house, not an Anglo-American interpretation of Palladio. The program enabled the architects to have symmetrical wing pavilions connected to the main house via arcaded hyphens, a characteristic device of Palladio. To anchor the house to the garden, an axial procession is established from the elevated entrance portico overlooking the front garden through a dramatically varied sequence of rooms to the two-story barrel-vaulted living room at the rear, opening out onto a loggia that culminates in the outdoor room of the garden's great central *tapis vert*. A pair of open terraces flanking the loggia—breakfast room and master bedroom suite terraces, respectively—offer *en-plein-air* enjoyment of the garden.

School in Rudrapur
Rudrapur, Bangladesh

Anna Heringer and Eike Roswag
Berlin, Germany

This school was hand-built in four months by local craftsmen, pupils, parents, and teachers together with experts and volunteers from Germany and Austria. It is located in the compound of a Bangladeshi non-governement organization, Dipshikha, which is dedicated to integrated and sustainable rural development. The philosophy of the school's educational program is "learning with joy," with an emphasis on helping the children to develop their own potential and use it in a creative way. The building follows the same principles, bringing out the best in local materials by inventively combining them with improved construction techniques. The lower portion consists of rammed-straw-reinforced mud walls finished with battered mud; the upper floor is a bamboo frame construction with slatted bamboo for the walls, windows, and doors; the roof is finished with sheets of corrugated galvanized metal.

Seaside Residence
Seaside, Florida, USA

Leo Casas
Seaside, Florida, USA

The Seaside Residence reflects the English heritage of the client and East Coast precedents easily acclimatized within the context of Seaside's residential neighborhood. The splendid corner lot gives the home a unique presence within the urban sequence through Seaside and its neighboring community. The stair tower on the corner establishes a formal urban marker within the public realm while providing the primary circulation and Gulf views for the home. The three-story porch on the front allows maximum viewable outdoor space toward the Gulf and provides a transition between public and private realms, typical of Seaside homes.

September 11th Memorial, Grosvenor Square
London, England

Russell Taylor Architects
London and Cornwall, England

This memorial takes the form of a garden, designed by Land Use Consultants, centered on a pavilion and embracing pergolas designed by the architect in a simple classical Tuscan style. Grosvenor Square was formed in the eighteenth century, and it seemed sensible to design a structure in harmony with the origins of the square as a classical temple in a garden landscape in keeping with the eighteenth-century picturesque landscape ideal. The pavilion and pergolas are constructed in green oak; each of the twenty-eight columns is a single tree trunk about 120 years old, cut to size, and carrying massive beams—it is a memorial designed to last. The columned temple form is a timeless type and perfectly appropriate to commemorate one of the most tragic events at the beginning of the twenty-first century.

Sidi Bou Said Houses
Sidi Bou Said, Tunisia

Tarak Ben Miled
Tunis, Tunisia

This project involves a number of reconstructed houses as well as new houses. The challenge was to create an architecture that blends new constructions with the scale and language of existing vernacular houses. The project encompasses both the urban and architectural scales. It successfully balances the harmonious emulation of urban reconstruction, sustainability of local materials, and use of local craftsmen all within a classical architectural tradition where the local and the universal are in permanent dialogue.

South Main
Buena Vista, Colorado, USA

Dover, Kohl & Partners
Coral Gables, Florida, USA

South Main is located in the Rocky Mountains in the heart of the Arkansas River Valley. It occupies a 38-acre site in the town of Buena Vista in Colorado. The founders of South Main envisioned their property as an environmentally friendly new neighborhood that would provide public access to both the riverfront and a world-class whitewater park. The master plan for the property connects the town of Buena Vista to the Arkansas River. Neighborhood streets are oriented to create views to the mountains as well as to the riverfront. The South Main Square, which abuts a new riverfront park, is surrounded by mixed-use buildings, and provides a central gathering space for residents and visitors. The project also features a variety of sustainable elements including a mix of uses and housing types employing locally influenced, time-tested architecture.

SOUTH MAIN
SOUTH MAIN ST

St. Albans School
Washington, D.C., USA

Jamshid Sepehri with Chatelain Architects
Washington, D.C., USA

The original southeast corner of Ralph Adams Cram's St. Albans school, of 1929, on the grounds of Washington National Cathedral, was altered in the 1950s. The new addition removed and replaced the 1950s facade with a load-bearing facade and corner tower that drew its inspiration from other of Cram's buildings. A rich palette of colors and textures combined with elegant and well-crafted details compose a sophisticated and compelling stone building, a testimony to the continuity and invention of contemporary traditional architecture.

Saint Margaret Mary Church
Bullhead City, Arizona

Duncan G. Stroik Architect
South Bend, Indiana, USA

Saint Margaret Mary is inspired by the mission churches of Mexico and the American Southwest. The church is located on a plateau next to existing parish buildings and can be seen from a great distance. An open courtyard provides an anteroom to the church and conceals some of the church's functions. The exterior of the church is finished in white stucco with a clay tile roof and a bell tower on the south side.

Saint Theresa Education Center
Sugar Land, Texas

Duncan G. Stroik Architect
South Bend, Indiana, USA

The Saint Theresa Education Center is the first phase of a master plan designed to revitalize the parish campus. The new building serves this parish in the Archdiocese of Houston in several ways: it houses a new elementary school for kindergarten through sixth grade, it provides offices for the parish staff, and it houses offices for catechetical education. The two-story brick and limestone building is inspired by Saint Mary Seminary and Ralph Adams Cram's buildings at Rice University.

St. Edward's Chapel, Casady School
Oklahoma City, Oklahoma, USA

Cram & Ferguson Architects
Concord, Massachusetts, USA

At St. Edward's Chapel at the Casady School, Cram & Ferguson Architects added new transepts and a tower to a church built by the firm in 1949. The new additions fulfill and complete the design intent of the original project. The west transept houses new office space and a sacristy, and in the east are located a reading room and smaller practice rooms. Both feature attached cloisters. The reading room includes a substantial new window with Gothic tracery and stained glass. The new 95-foot tower includes a twenty-three-bell carillon. New slate shingles and insulation were added to the roof of the existing structure. Replacing a set of out-of-character aluminum doors, new wooden doors were fabricated from the original drawings and details to restore the intended appearance of the building.

St. Erik Crescent
Stockholm, Sweden

Brunnberg & Forshed Arkitektkontor
Stockholm, Sweden

This development features seven hundred new homes and the preservation of older buildings on a former hospital campus (St. Erik) in the heart of downtown Stockholm. The crescent embraces the old hospital park, which still has many beautiful trees. The buildings are built in a durable manner and characterized by vertical window proportions, glazed verandas, and red-tiled roofs. The project has been developed in collaboration and coordination with Stockholm's urban planning department.

Summer Palace
Peterhof, Russia

Ivan Kniazev and Irina Efendieva
Saint Petersburg, Russia

The Summer Palace is a new banqueting hall for a hotel and a large restaurant located in Peterhof, widely known as a Baroque core of the chain of imperial residences along the south bank of the Finnish Gulf. The Baroque character of the place has become one of the major reasons for its attractiveness and success.
It seemed natural to refer to the traditions of both Baroque and neo-Palladian revival as well as to works by Antonio Rinaldi, Vincenzo Brenna, and Vasili Bazhenov as the main precedents for the Summer Palace. The modest exterior with brick stucco walls was enhanced with a sculpture, *Fortune*, by artists Pavel Ignatiev and Denis Prasolov and by decorative vases with modified moldings from a restored monument by Antonio Rinaldi. The interiors are characterized by excellent decorative arts in the classical tradition done by artists graduating from the St. Petersburg Academy of Fine Arts.

't Haegsch Hof, Rivierenbuurt
The Hague, Netherlands

K & K Architekten
Berlin, Germany

In The Hague, 't Haegsch, Rivierenbuurt, a new urban complex with around two hundred dwellings, has been built on the area of the former state printing works south of the political and cultural center of the city. The core of Rivierenbuurt is a funnel-shaped public square that opens toward the canal. The square is accentuated by a generous water area and an octagonal eight-floor-high apartment tower. The individually designed and impressive facades of the houses are modeled on historical local archetypes.

The American School in Switzerland
Lugano, Switzerland

David Mayernik
South Bend, Indiana, USA

This project comprises a comprehensive, long-term plan of development for the campus of The American School in Switzerland. It balances open green space on the campus's precious flatground while developing a village environment on the hillside for the school's academic, sports, and residence functions. Each building is an articulate part of the dialogue between buildings of an urban ensemble and positive open space: they both represent their role and place in the school's life while shaping a pedestrian-oriented environment of passages, piazzas, and stairways.

The Palladium
Carmel, Indiana, USA

David M. Schwarz Architects
Washington, D.C., USA

The Palladium at the Center for the Performing Arts is the focal point of a large, new mixed-use city center development project comprised of office, retail, residential, and hotel space.

Like the Villa Rotonda by Andrea Palladio, the building is centrally planned with four equally weighted wings projecting from a central domed rotunda in order to respond equally to important neighboring development. Major entrances are incorporated into the south, east, and west wings. The three entrances open to double-height lobbies that are connected to one another by generous stair passages and elevators.

The exterior is clad in Indiana limestone and is detailed in a traditional architectural vocabulary stylized and refined to mark the perpetual freshness and inventiveness within the classical tradition. Stylized geometric brackets support deep horizontal projecting cornices and all window and door openings are treated with robust ornamental surrounds. The concert hall features a large elliptical dome with a central oculus. The room is extended at both ends by half circle alcoves that contain balcony audience seating to the south and the performance platform, choral terrace, and concert organ to the north. The architectural details in the hall are exposed to natural lighting provided by a glass and steel canopy that reads as a piece of theatrical setting.

Villa
Bidaa, Kuwait

Alidad
London, England

The interiors of this new villa were designed with the aim of creating classically proportioned rooms and volumes from the trapezium-shaped plan that is dictated by the shape of the plot. The orthogonal and polygonal rooms are arranged in harmonious sequence mediated by the *poche* spaces left by the periphery and outline of the plan. The most ingenious outcome, which demonstrates the classical sensibility of the designer, is perhaps the creation of a cloakroom that resolves the clash of several geometries into the harmony of an octagon. The exteriors of the villa, designed by Alireza Sagharchi of Stanhope Gate Architecture, offered splendid opportunities for celebrating the synthesis of interiors and its dialogue with the classical tectonics and ornament of the exterior. The interiors of the villa are composed as a procession of grand and perfectly balanced rooms that lead one from a large entrance hall to a double-height main hall surmounted with a coffered dome, a salon, a library, and a luxurious *triclinium* lined with Italian marble columns.

Tommy Hilfiger Flagship Store
Beverly Hills, California

Allan Greenberg Architect
Alexandria, Virginia; Greenwich, Connecticut; New York, New York, USA

This retail project was conceived to establish a West Coast presence for New York fashion designer Tommy Hilfiger (it is currently occupied by Brooks Brothers). Located at the prime Beverly Hills intersection of Rodeo Drive and Little Santa Monica Boulevard, the store was designed in close collaboration with the local community and the owner. The gleaming white two-story facade echoes the clothing designer's personality, "a bold yet civilized twist," using the language of nineteenth-century market architecture. A second-floor balcony with an elaborately detailed pergola overlooks the street. With its strong detailing and interplay of light and shadow, the building's monochromatic design enhances the street context, enriches the local civic character, and provides interest during the day and at night. The building features large display windows and a dramatic two-story staircase with a large skylight and cupola

above. All elements combine to reflect the owner's desire for a strong connection between street and exterior.

Tottenham Court Road
London, England

Quinlan & Francis Terry Architects
Dedham, Surrey, England

The new development at 264–267 Tottenham Court Road, on St. Giles Circus in London, replaces a nineteenth-century building in the French Chateau style. Many schemes were proposed for the site, and at the suggestion of the planners it was decided that classical detailing would be appropriate to follow the example of many fine twentieth-century classical buildings on Oxford Street. The building is a mixed-use development with the ground floor used for retail, the next four floors offices, and residential units at roof level.

The elevation facing Tottenham Court Road is a nine-bay classical building 100 feet wide in natural limestone, bronze, and glass, in keeping with the buildings on either side, which are also constructed in Portland stone, glass, and bronze. This composition starts at ground level with a rusticated arcade supporting a giant Palladian Ionic order, with a superimposed giant Corinthian order above, complete with entablature, balustrade, an attic, and a slate roof behind the parapet. The detailing of the column capitals, bases, and cornices are all from Palladio's *Quattro Libri*. At the two ends of the colonnade are plain rusticated bookends that frame the composition and make a clean joint with the neighboring classical buildings on either side.

265
WE WILL ROCK YOU
GARFUNKEL'S

Touma House
Damascus, Syria

Antoine Touma
Damascus, Syria

This suburban house attempts to set an example for integrating traditional patterns, materials, and techniques in the context of a sustainable modernity, cultural identity, and sense of place. It takes as its model a Damascene courtyard house, but, following the convention for hillside houses, the fourth side is opened to the landscape, with an arcade offering generous views. Careful research identified appropriate features, such as the sheltering *iwans* on each side of the court. Emphasis was placed on reviving dying crafts, with industrialized materials like aluminium and plastic and oil-derived by-products discarded in favor of local wood and stone, including pink granite salvaged from derelict buildings. Double external walls make air-conditioning redundant and provide space for traditional features such as niches and shutters.

Tree House
Cheshire, North Carolina, USA

Seth Harry & Associates
Baltimore, Maryland, USA

This project is located in the traditional neighborhood development of Cheshire, outside of Black Mountain, North Carolina. The design concept was developed from a pioneering house type, known as "tree houses" because of their unique characteristics of small footprints (20 feet by 20 feet) stacked three stories high to preserve existing trees and topography. The architecture of the house takes its inspiration from the Arts and Crafts style of traditional architecture, which is prevalent in the area.

Villa Boim, Monte da Herdade do Rego
Elvas, Alentejo, Portugal

José Baganha & Arquitectos Associados
Lisbon, Portugal

The series of buildings normally comprising the main house, buildings for permanent or temporary farm employees, and the annexes for storing equipment is customarily called a *monte* in the Alentejo region of Southern Portugal. The *monte* of this property, the Herdade do Rego, was run-down when the current owners decided to renovate the buildings. The type of construction, using lath-and-plaster walls and pantile roof tiles laid on timber beams, is very characteristic of the region. The solid architecture of the old house still displays its durability and blends perfectly with the land. The overall impression of the *monte* and the surrounding landscape is such that one could not exist without the other. Old and new are integrated using the same architectural approach, the same typology, making the best use of the building and providing it with the utmost comfort and solidity.

Villa Borelli
Fornovo di Taro, Italy

Pier Carlo Bontempi Architects
Parma, Italy

Villa Borelli is a villa in the best sense as it is designed to both satisfy the needs of agricultural activities and the delights of the typical *villeggiatura*, of leisure and cultivated *otium* away from the business and stress of urban life. Villa in its original meaning refers in fact to an organic whole consisting of farmlands, landscaped gardens, and a variety of buildings serving to sustain both a complex territorial economy and a refined social and cultural life. Located on a sunny plateau between the hills of vineyards famous for their Sauvignon grapes, the villa is formed by an organic ensemble of buildings nestled in the countryside along a little country road. The main house is in the classical style with a generous loggia looking out to the west. Other more rustic utilitarian buildings, such as wine cellars and service buildings are built in stone and bricks and are vernacular in character.

Villa Gemma
Alba Adriatica, Italy

Luigi del Sordo
Alba Adriatica, Italy

Located in an existing garden, Villa Gemma defers to both its site and local building traditions to create an exquisite synthesis of nature and architecture. The location of the main building, terraces, porches, pool pavilion, and garden pavilions are carefully arranged in order to merge with the mature pine, palm, and linden trees that frame spectacular views of the nearby hills, olive gardens, and vineyards. Built with bricks produced locally with clays and travertine stone from neighboring Ascoli, it takes its architectural inspiration both from numerous local precedents in classical and vernacular architecture and the handbooks and treatises used by craftsmen and architects in previous centuries. The buildings are articulated in simple and clear volumes organized by subtle local symmetries and punctuated with well-crafted classical elements and details. The interiors are generously laid out with a clear and spacious plan and decorated

tastefully with art works and traditional ornaments in travertine and painted majolica. Villa Gemma achieves a delightful synthesis between interiors and outdoor spaces with life, joy, and harmony delicately expressed in the poetics of architecture.

Villas in Germany
Berlin and Munich, Germany

Hans Kollhoff Architekten
Berlin, Germany, and Zurich, Switzerland

The design of villas was an uncomfortable topic of German postwar architecture. Only Julius Posener succeeded in reminding a younger generation of the great villas by Muthesius and the influence of Schinkel's country houses in the work of Peter Behrens, Bruno Paul, and Mies van der Rohe. Villas have always been iconic and influential as they often seem to illustrate most effectively the synergy between the latest theory and best practices, between the spirit of time and the *genius loci*.

Villa G. is located in Berlin-Dahlem, a historical suburban villa area in Berlin. It is characterized by an almost cubist architecture, with a restrained and precise composition achieving a monolithic quality stressed by the stucco facade. The symmetrical composition with a central entrance and stair hall is reinforced by the corner pavilions. The rigor and purity of the exterior, enhancing a more public character of the villa, is contrasted by interiors focusing on the intimacy and privacy of family life.

Villa D. is located on a narrow lot in a historical preservation area in Munich. Its individuality derives from a classical reformulation of the more picturesque suburban villa. The almost monolithic severity is enriched by generous references to traditional precedents with opulent roofs, white windows, and green shutters perfectly crafted in timber, and a subtle facade treatment using stucco and stone. Villa D. is well integrated in its historic context. It appears to have been there forever.

William Wake House
Northampton, England

Robert Adam, ADAM Architecture
Winchester, England

William Wake House is a substantial purpose-built hospital unit for St. Andrew's Healthcare, thought to be the largest classical new building in Britain in over fifty years. It has been designed with health-building experts Oxford Architects to include courtyards and internal spaces, and provides facilities that aid treatment and rehabilitation while offering an appropriate level of safety and security. The outer form and facade of the building is in keeping with the original hospital buildings, designed by George Wallet in 1835. The 170-meter-long principal elevations are broken up into a series of individual pavilions reflecting the organization of the internal plan. The external walls are in stucco and stone with a slate roof. Interior courtyards are designed with simplified classical detailing in two colors of brick.

Whittlebury Lodge
Northamptonshire, England

Peregrine Bryant
London, England

In the English tradition of the small country house or hunting lodge, Whittlebury Lodge was designed to sit naturally in the contours and features of the existing landscape of an ancient deer park. The design is consistent with the enduring Palladian model of the simple country villa while ensuring its use as a practical family home suited to modern needs. It provides family accommodation within a three-story central block with two one-and-a-half-story ancillary wings. Internally the design reflects twenty-first-century life, and subtle attention is drawn to the hierarchy of the rooms within the house through classical architectural detailing. It is one of the few built examples of houses granted planning permission within the green belt land in England. The planning policy was brought about in 1997 to allow isolated new houses in the countryside that "are truly outstanding in terms of architecture and landscape design and would significantly enhance their immediate setting and wider surroundings." The house is built in traditional load-bearing construction and lime rendered in a soft ochre color over brick with stone dressings.

Wyatt Residence
Pittsburgh, Pennsylvania, USA

Alvin Holm Architects
Philadelphia, Pennsylvania, USA

The Wyatt Residence is a house in the hills outside of Pittsburgh designed in the neo-Georgian manner. The house is based on Palladio's Villa Rotonda as desired by the architect and suggested by the potential of the site with a strong influence introduced by the client. The inspiration from Italian and English precedents and the references to a solid European and American classical tradition concluded successfully in an authentic American villa.

Yakup Içgören House
Bodrum, Turkey

Ahmet Igdirligil
Bodrum, Turkey

This single-unit home in Bodrum, expanded with an addition of a kitchen and bathroom block, creates an updated typology perfectly responding to issues of context and identity as well as modern comfort. Taking advantage of the topography and consistent with traditional patterns for houses, the architect articulated the various domestic activities over various levels according to the functional requirements and local cultural practices and domestic rituals. Outdoor patios and terraces on the north and the south complement and enhance climatic comfort and offer spectacular views of the landscape as well as intimate shaded areas. The guest room is designed as an independent unit in keeping with the proportions of the main structure in order to maximize use of external spaces. The buildings are constructed in traditional load-bearing stone walls with most of the stone obtained from a local quarry.

From Apologia to Praxis

Three Generations of New Traditional Architects

Richard M. Economakis

Proposed new Whitmore Hotel, Bath, north facade facing existing Victoria Park. The hotel is named after Regency architect George Whitmore, architect of the Palace of St. Michael and St. George in Corfu. Designed by the University of Notre Dame Bath Summer Studio, 2009.

When modern traditional architecture emerged again in the late 1970s, there were no dedicated schools or institutions to enlighten and support its advocates. The first generation of practitioners was one of autodidacts, who by careful observation of older buildings and cities and immersion in neglected literature, documents, and records succeeded in recovering the elements of language and those principles of composition that for centuries before the rise of Modernism[1] were understood to constitute the basis of good architecture. There have been other resurgences of classical architecture, but none in such a negatively charged atmosphere. When Alberti put pen to paper in the early fifteenth century, the thread of continuity since Roman times had been severed, but the notion of its restitution was not dismissed or put down by the cultural establishment; instead, it was welcomed as a necessary restoration of an urbane, civilizing culture of building. By contrast, the writings and work of first-generation modern classicists have been forged in a spirit of *apologia*, and tend to focus attention especially on those areas where they most profoundly diverge from mainstream practice. This is natural, for it was incumbent on those architects to demonstrate that the principles by which they now chose instead to abide, although discarded by the profession decades earlier, retain meaning and relevance in the modern age; indeed, that they represent a far more sensible approach to the making of shelter than what was then—and still is—being promoted by the establishment. Thus the "first wave" of traditional architects was primarily one of *exegetes* and polemicists, who recognized that the task before them involved much more than the re-espousal of pre-Modernist formal approaches. They needed to show that, unlike Modernist creations, traditional buildings and cities are both natural and intrinsically urbane; and that they need to be embraced again if the terrible process of urban, social, and environmental degeneration is to be reversed. The new traditional, or classical,[2] vision was understood to be an all-encompassing and global project; it is, as Léon Krier put it, ultimately an *ecological* undertaking.

Krier and other intellectually minded members of his generation established a broad conceptual framework for the new traditional architecture, which identifies and embraces those principles of order and common sense that give pre-Modernist cities and buildings their eminently humane qualities. Older formal strategies were cast in the fresh light of contemporary culture and viewed through a critical retrospective lens; innovation, which builds on prior accomplishment, now replaced invention as the principal tool for change. We owe to Krier our renewed understanding of the traditional city as comprising walkable, mixed-use neighborhoods, with distinct yet integrated public and private realms; a hierarchy of civic, commercial, and residential components; and expressions that range from vernacular to monumental depending on the purpose of the building.[3] Demetri Porphyrios undertook to explain the tectonic nature of classical forms: their rootedness, in other words, in robust building traditions, and the importance to architecture of the notions of imitation and ideality.[4] Allan Greenberg reminded us of the origin of classical forms and building types in the free exchange of ideas that is fostered in a democratically governed society.[5] These building types were described by Carroll William Westfall as the basic constituent elements of a healthy polity, which cares for its citizens by facilitating a range of civic activities and providing appropriate forms of shelter.[6] Shadowing these thinkers at every turn—and contributing through his own theoretical reflections—architectural historian David Watkin has ensured that their arguments make their way into the narrative of contemporary architecture,[7] alongside the work of influential historical figures, which he reexamines from a classical vantage point, his writings being mercifully free of the familiar attempts to place pre-twentieth-century architects into a Modernist developmental sequence.

First generation classicist John Blatteau helped to reintroduce rigor in the design of buildings by instructing his designers in the art of watercolor rendering as it was once taught at the École des Beaux-Arts.[8] This technique has taken root again at the University of Notre Dame, the Institute for Classical Architecture (ICA), and in numerous dedicated private practices.[9] Quinlan Terry, Abdel-Wahed El-Wakil, John Simpson, and a handful of other practitioners demonstrated that traditional techniques and craftsmanship can be brought back and relied upon again today. At the same time, Porphyrios, Robert Adam, Robert A. M. Stern, Andrés Duany, Elizabeth Plater-Zyberk, and others have shown (though not always entirely convincingly) that some "modern" materials and even certain Modernist sensibilities may yet have a role to play in the making of new classical buildings. The efforts of these professionals were aided by two adventurous publishing ventures, Maurice Culot's AAM in France, and Andreas Papadakis's Academy Editions in Britain. These outfits broke the "seal of silence" that had greeted new traditional architecture and prevented it from reaching the public. Culot and Papadakis fostered debate within the profession and prompted traditional architects to articulate their position and thereby attain legitimacy within intellectual circles. The justification of the classical/traditional viewpoint soon opened doors to positions of authority (albeit limited), which led to the establishment of schools, research institutes, and professional organizations. Some of these would succumb to mainstream resistance or poor management,[10] but most have continued to grow and play an important role in promoting classical and traditional architecture.

The 1990s and the first decade of the twenty-first century was a period of consolidation and growth for the new traditional architecture. Budding professional organizations and educational or academic institutions were energized by a dedicated "second wave" of architects who had gained experience in first-generation offices. Like their employers, these designers had not benefited from a formal classical education, but most were carefully trained by their mentors, who sometimes even put them through rigorous academic-type exercises. This "in-house" schooling helped to ensure competency and continuity in the workplace and made up for the absence of qualified professional recruits. Some apprentices shared their employers' sense of mission and soon ventured into the public arena as independent professionals or authors of valuable essays and books, competition entries, and counter-projects. Others chose to hitch their careers to their professional outfits, rising to the level of associate and sometimes even partner.

Whether operating independently or in partnership, second-generation traditional architects were instrumental in establishing highly competitive professional practices, which has bolstered confidence across the ranks. The inroads made by this second wave have very much to do with its attitude toward the establishment. Its members no longer see themselves as a "salon des refusés" but instead as a *bona fide* branch of the profession. They have learned to be vocal without nursing grudges, helping themselves in the absence of reliable support from within the profession, while keeping the more hostile mainstream elements in their place with reminders of the tolerance and inclusivity promised by the present age of pluralism. This of course has not guaranteed fair play—witness, for instance, the composition of juries in important public competitions, which still only very rarely include traditional architects—but it has made for a more civil professional environment. It is significant that most traditional offices are at the top of their profession in terms of solvency and the quality of the services they provide, whereas relatively few Modernist practices achieve a comparable level of success.

A strong sense of professionalism also characterizes the intellectual, academic, and other activities of second-generation traditional architects, whose writings have been helped by a few steadfast journals like *The Classicist*, *American Arts Quarterly*, and Clem Labine's *Traditional Building* magazine, and a handful of publishing houses that continue periodically to produce titles on historic and contemporary traditional subjects and architects. Architectural historian, and former director of the Prince of Wales's Institute of Architecture, Richard John has published extensive monographs on the work of first-generation classicists John Simpson, Robert Adam, and Thomas Gordon Smith, and these join a growing number of useful office publications and surveys of contemporary traditional work.[11] Among the latter, the books *New Classicism* by Elizabeth Meredith Dowling,[12] the ICA's *A Decade of Art & Architecture, 1992–2002*,[13] and *New Palladians* by Alireza Sagharchi and Lucien Steil[14] stand out for their breadth and emphasis on quality in design.[15]

Ground has also been gained in the area of historical research, with new publications that discuss pre-Modernist works not as interesting but otherwise irrelevant artifacts of the past but instead as useful precedents for contemporary work. New Zealand–based academic Branko Mitrović has cast new light on the architecture of the Italian Renaissance with his discerning studies of the architecture and writings of Palladio and Vignola.[16] These works complement the new masterful translation of Vitruvius by Ingrid Rowland[17] and richly illustrated edition of *The Ten Books* by Thomas Gordon Smith.[18] Closer to home, the work of nineteenth- and early-twentieth-century classicists Delano and Aldrich, Warren and Wetmore, Grosvenor Atterbury, and others has been meticulously researched and published by second-generation classicist Peter Pennoyer and architectural historian Anne Walker,[19] who contribute to an expanding list of monographs on other significant architects of this period, including McKim, Mead, and White, David Adler, Daniel Burnham, Philip Trammell Shutze, and John Russell Pope. In a similar vein, traditional architect Marc Appleton has reintroduced the work of George Washington Smith, a California architect and painter who helped to popularize Spanish Colonial Revival architecture, especially in Santa Barbara;[20] and Jeffrey Tilman has rekindled the legacy of another West Coast architect of the early twentieth century, Arthur Brown Jr., who built the San Francisco City Hall, Memorial Opera House, and other well-known civic edifices in the first half of the twentieth century.[21]

Lesser-known nineteenth- and early-twentieth-century architects George Whitmore and Albert Simons have been brought to the profession's attention in articles by this essayist and academic Ralph Muldrow,[22] and the writings and architecture of Sir Reginald Blomfield have been carefully sifted through by Katherine Wheeler. The even less familiar but steadfastly traditional work of José Allegue, a Spanish immigrant builder who worked in southwestern Long Island between 1928 and 1968, and who remained steadfastly traditional despite the profession's espousal of Modernist approaches, is carefully documented in an elegant book produced by architect Christine Franck.[23] The work of Frenchman Pierre Barbe, another early apostate from Modernism, has been painstakingly researched by Jean-Baptiste Minnaert[24] and given its due place in the history of what Michael Lykoudis, dean of the School of Architecture at the University of Notre Dame, has called "the other modern." Architectural historian Lucy Archer has done the same for Raymond Erith,[25] a discerning English architect and voice of dissent during the 1950s and 1960s. The list of such publications continues to grow as the work and writings of accomplished traditional architects from the periods immediately preceding and following the rise of Modernism are brought again into the limelight.

Supplementing these various studies are a slew of new reprints of important eighteenth-, nineteenth-, and early-twentieth-century manuals on the language of classical architecture, including valuable Dover editions of Sir William Chambers's *Treatise on Civil Architecture* (1759),[26] Nathaniel C. Curtis's *Architectural Composition* (1926),[27] and Arthur Stratton's *Elements of Form and Design in Classic Architecture* (1925).[28] A number of these guidebooks feature preambles by second-generation traditional architects; for instance, Mauch and Normand's *Parallel of the Classical Orders of Architecture* is introduced by architect and founding member of the ICA, Donald Rattner,[29] who explains the relevance of the plates to the modern reader. Richard Sammons, also a founding member of the ICA and principal of the firm Fairfax & Sammons, was instrumental in producing new editions of the books *The Elements of Classical Architecture* by Georges Gromort (1910),[30] and *Theory of Mouldings* by C. Howard Walker (1926), for which he has written a foreword.[31] These publications follow on earlier reprints like William Ware's *The American Vignola: A Guide to the Making of Classical Architecture*, which featured a preface by Arthur Ross and introductory notes by John Barrington Bayley and Henry Hope Reed;[32] and Hector D'Espouy's *Fragments d'Architecture Antique*, with introductory notes by John Blatteau.[33] Furthering this genre, a number of useful new manuals on classical architecture have appeared,[34] including *Classical Architecture* by Robert Adam,[35] *The Architecture of the Classical Interior* by Steven Semes,[36] and *Classical Architecture for the Twenty First Century* by Jean-François Gabriel.[37]

Some "in-betweeners," as one architect has teasingly called his second generation, have furthered the foundational arguments put forward by Krier, Porphyrios, Westfall, Watkin, and other first-generation theorists and historians. For instance, in *The True, the Fictive, and the Real: The Historical Dictionary of Architecture of Quatremère de Quincy*,[38] Samir Younés traces the sources of the new classical understanding of such notions as imitation, invention, the tectonic order, character, and type in architecture to the writings of eighteenth-century French architect Antoine-Chrysostôme Quatremère de Quincy, and ultimately to Greek Platonic thinking. When, in his thoughtful tour of Renaissance Italy, *Timeless Cities*,[39] David Mayernik wonders "if we could imagine a city built to articulate political virtues rather than political systems or techniques," he does more than echo Westfall's admonition that politics trumps architecture; he nudges us, in effect, beyond politics, to "remove the mission of civic architecture from pure pragmatics and give back to it some kind of a transcendent value system." Only then, he argues, will we "find our way back to the culture of Florentine civic humanists." Others have endeavored to extend the discussion of the role of tradition into important related fields such as historic preservation and the environment. In his book *The Future of the Past*,[40] Steven W. Semes questions Modernist attitudes toward the restoration and extension of historic buildings that were promoted by the Venice Charter of 1964, a document that strongly influenced the U.S. secretary of the interior's Standards for Rehabilitation of 1977 and has been adopted as law by countries around the world, arguing that interventions of any sort should properly respect the style and character of the older edifices that they purport to enhance.

Members of the second generation of new traditional architects have played an important role in establishing prestigious awards like the European Prize for the Reconstruction of the City, the Arthur Ross and Palladio Awards, the Stanford White Award, the Newington-Cropsey Award, CNU Charter Awards, and the Henry Hope Reed Award and Richard A. Driehaus Prize, the latter carrying the largest cash reward currently offered in the architectural world. They have also come to staff organizations like the School of Architecture at the University of Notre Dame in Indiana (the first fully accredited program in classical architecture, begun under the chairmanship of Thomas Gordon Smith, and currently headed by Dean Michael Lykoudis[41]), the Prince of Wales's Institute of Architecture in London (now the Prince's Foundation for the Arts), Classical America and the Institute of Classical Architecture (which merged to become the ICA & CA, and is now officially the ICAA), the Charter for the New Urbanism, INTBAU, the Traditional Architecture Group (TAG, now a bona fide branch of the Royal Institute of British Architects chaired by Alireza Sagharchi), etc. Among the various activities of these educators, one of the most important has been the organization of task forces in cities around the world, with the purpose of developing strategies for their proper reconstruction and development.

Master plan proposals have been produced by the Prince's Foundation for cities in Lebanon, Saudi Arabia, Germany, Britain, the United States, Jamaica, Sierra Leone, Haiti, China, and elsewhere.[42] University of Notre Dame faculty have led master plan efforts in Italy, Greece, the United States, Britain, and Cuba: in the summer of 2009, students under the direction of this essay's author and then-visiting professor Samantha Salden studied the city of Bath and produced a counterproposal for the Western Riverside area, which is threatened by insensitive Modernist-inspired development;[43] in 2011, a master plan proposal for Skaneateles, New York, by students of Notre Dame's director of graduate studies Philip Bess, received the CNU's 2011 Academic grand prize;[44] even more recently, visiting professors Luis and Jorge Trelles traveled with a team of students to Havana, where, with the assistance of University of Miami faculty members Rafael Fornes, Teófilo Victoria, and others, they laid down the first guidelines for the city's growth according to traditional principles.[45] At the University of Miami, charrettes in the U.S., Europe, Mexico, the Dominican Republic, and elsewhere have been organized by the Center for Urban and Community Design and Knight Program, and new campaigns are yet being planned. Comparable efforts are being made by faculty at the University of Maryland, Andrews University (impressively, Urban

Design Studio Director Andrew von Maur's charrette projects have received four consecutive CNU Awards), and other schools where second-generation traditional architects have found welcoming academic environments. These academic exercises are important for the guidance they offer to local communities, as well as for the insights they provide to students into the complex range of urban and architectural problems faced by cities today. These students are members an emerging "third wave" of classical and traditional architects, the contributions of which have already significantly impacted the movement and are being felt by the profession at large.

This new generation is being shaped under manifestly different circumstances. For one thing, it is not self-taught, nor has it been exposed to the process of critical self-realization that its mentors and teachers had been before them. The case for rejecting Modernism had already been spelled out by the 1990s and tends to be presented to them as *credo*. Thus the benefits of a classical education are sometimes tempered by a desire to "know the other side," or else by a false sense of normalcy, when in fact traditional architecture still has a good way to go before it can feel entirely welcome in the professional arena. Furthermore, unlike the previous two generations, many talented young classicists setting out in "the real world" can aspire to pursue conventional careers in traditional firms or in offices that include traditional work as part of their repertoire.[46] Some of these practices are run by seasoned first- and second-generation architects, who still take it upon themselves occasionally to skirmish with the establishment; most, however, are operated by quiet professionals who have either been compelled more recently to embrace traditional architecture or have chosen to respond to the growing demand for traditional work and rely on classically educated or trained staff to ensure quality in their work. The proliferation of traditional firms in the last ten years is certainly auspicious and reflects the steadily growing interest of the public in classical and traditional work. A number of practices have even come to be thought of as extensions of the university studio and classroom; places where classical designers can further the skills and knowledge they acquired in academia (or "the academy," if their experience was obtained at the ICA, the Prince of Wales's Institute, or other learning centers that do not have university accreditation). The sense of security and professional "normalcy" that these environments instill, however, coupled with understandable time-management and conflict-of-interest provisos, tend to dampen the youthful appetite for taking on the larger issues of the day individually. There is a sense, too, that what needs to be said about classical and traditional architecture has already been adequately stated. The prevailing sense among younger traditional architects, therefore, is that their contribution will be judged less on the basis of intellectual argument and *exegesis*, and more on output and fastidiousness or exactitude in design; in other words, on *praxis*.

Good examples of practical thinking among the younger ranks and recent converts to traditional architecture are found in the handbooks *Get Your House Right* by Marianne Cusato and Ben Pentreath (with Richard Sammons and Léon Krier),[47] and *Traditional Construction Patterns* by Stephen A. Mouzon,[48] which go a step further than the manuals by Adam, Semes, Gabriel, etc., by providing detailed instructions—including lists of "dos" and "don'ts"—for architects as much as for builders and developers. This genre of publication is echoed in the pattern books produced by New Urbanist offices, most notably the Pittsburgh firm Urban Design Associates, a number of which have been endorsed by state governors, mayors, and other high-ranking members of the civil service.[49] The increasing ability to persuade and win over members of the political establishment is in fact indicative not just of a new outlook among traditional architects but of an improving attitude toward them within the profession. Third-generation professionals in particular have been helped in this by a combination of confidence and "philosophical levity," the latter deriving from the strangeness of being ignored by their own profession for advocating what until a handful of decades ago had been considered proper to the art of building. Perhaps more even than their talent and expertise, this self-deprecating assurance has earned younger traditional architects many new friends and allies.

It has also turned former opponents into sympathetic or at least forbearing rivals: these turned up in droves at the *Three Architects* exhibition held at the RIBA in London in May 2010, which featured the work of third-generationers Ben Pentreath, George Saumarez Smith, and Francis Terry. In his description of the exhibit that was published in the *RIBA Journal*, noted British architecture critic and establishment mouthpiece Hugh Pearman shows more than mere tolerance for this trio of young classicists: he speaks of them as representatives of a recognized strand in a "necessarily pluralist" profession.[50] "Although distinctly self-mocking," says Pearman of the young architects, "they believe with absolute seriousness in the rightness and quality of the work they do." The relaxed, playful—what Pearman describes as "tongue-in-cheek"—attitude of the three exhibitors typifies the emerging generation of traditional architects and has helped to break the ice that had built up between the Modernist mainstream and defiant first-generation classicists.

The pragmatic outlook of this third generation sometimes comes through as a fully fledged entrepreneurial spirit. For instance, Marianne Cusato's Katrina Cottage initiative originally involved collaboration with a major home improvement store to promote traditional small house designs that could serve as low-cost shelters for families that were displaced in the wake of Hurricane Katrina in 2005. The cottages are designed as easily assembled building kits that range from just over 300 to 1,300 square feet in floor area. The buildings meet the International Building Code and most hurricane codes, and remain popular with families seeking affordable housing both in storm-ravaged areas and elsewhere as modest domiciles. Another example of healthy commercial instincts among younger practitioners is found in Ben Pentreath's thriving home furnishings shop, which he set up with decorative artist Bridie Hall in London's Bloomsbury in 2008 as an extension of his architectural practice in nearby Lamb's Conduit Street.[51] This venture resembles the dedicated builders' supply stores that proliferated in eighteenth- and nineteenth-century Britain, serving prospective homeowners and developers. In this connection we may also cite David Harlan's custom furniture business,[52] Michael Imber's interior design operation,[53] David Mayernik's fresco and decorative arts practice, and more.

An enterprising spirit likewise prompted Notre Dame architecture librarian Jennifer Parker to collaborate with the university's Hesburgh Libraries and architecture faculty member Samantha Salden in 2011 to create the Seaside Research Portal, an innovative interactive digital archive that allows visitors access to the entire history of the new town's growth, from its inception by Robert Davis in 1978 to the first master plan by Andrés Duany and Elizabeth Plater-Zyberk and its subsequent development.[54] A few doors down and across from Salden's office, another academic, INTBAU-India chair Krupali Krusche, is exploiting contemporary technology in a different but equally industrious way, spearheading a digital research and documentation project (DHARMA) to document World Heritage sites, including the Taj Mahal and Roman Forum. This last site has been separately and beautifully reconstructed through a combination of digital and traditional rendering techniques by Krusche's Notre Dame colleague Gil Gorski, an architect and architectural illustrator.[55] Third-generation traditional architects are also extending their attention to the critical issues of building technology, sustainability, and the environment. Through her "Green Scale" research project,[56] Notre Dame academic Aimee Buccellato has been researching digital methods of quantifying the inherently durable and sustainable characteristics of traditional building materials and techniques, an effort which promises to greatly reinforce the new traditional position through scientific fact-finding. At Cornell University, classically trained architect and now academic Kim Rollings has studied the effect of the built environment on human well-being, drawing conclusions that corroborate the argument that traditional urban settings are healthier places from a medical point of view.[57] Research in these and other areas relating to the concerns of new traditional architecture continues to develop, perhaps not yet in leaps and bounds, but steadily and admirably on the strength of the commitment of these architect-turned-scientists/technicians.

If the quality of traditional work has improved in the last couple of decades, it is due in large part to third-generation input.[58] The classical vocabulary of forms is often handled expertly; vernacular compositions are carefully balanced; architectural details reveal a proper understanding of tectonic principles; in general, building design has reached a level of sophistication comparable to pre-Modernist work. All this can be said to make up in some degree for the slowing of intellectual discourse in the last fifteen years or so. There are a few areas, however, that need special attention, if traditional architects are to maintain credibility in the eyes of the profession. These are: a lackadaisical attitude by many practitioners toward the shaping of the urban context; an inclination to think generically in terms of styles, which are sometimes used inappropriately in their given context rather than in terms of genuinely regional expressions that can be creatively manipulated; and a resignation to the use of modern materials and techniques.

A lackadaisical attitude by many practitioners toward the shaping of the urban context: Some of the more accomplished new traditional buildings burrow in exclusive suburbs and gated "neighborhoods" that turn their backs on the village or town; or, if no *urbs* are to be found in the vicinity, they do little to encourage their proper development. One cannot, of course, blame traditional architects for taking on commissions in exclusive "communities," especially when livelihoods must be earned under the present unfavorable circumstances. They must, however, take care not to lapse into complacency with regard to the continuing process of suburbanization and fragmentation of the city. As specialists they owe it to themselves as much as to the world to edify their clients as to the full extent of their vision, especially its urban, social, and environmental implications. If physicians are expected to swear by the Hippocratic oath, and thereby acknowledge a moral dimension in their work, or if lawyers are required to abide by standards of ethics, so should traditional architects, whose vision, if it is to have any consequence, depends on a commitment to reconstruct the integrated city of neighborhoods, take it on as an obligation to advise clients and municipal authorities on the appropriate development of sites. One such undertaking that yielded felicitous results was the development of the new town of Cayalá in Guatemala. Here the client originally envisaged a chain of gated suburban enclaves comprising clusters of villas and residential towers but was persuaded to adopt a traditional urban model in response to appeals by traditional architects Pedro Pablo Godoy, Maria Sánchez, and others, including the project's master-planner, Léon Krier.[59] The scheme, currently in its third stage of implementation, places the high-end residences within the urban fabric and at walking distance from the public spaces, without compromising the required lot sizes and floor areas, security and privacy requirements, views, etc.

An inclination to think generically in terms of styles, which are sometimes used inappropriately in their given context, rather than in terms of genuinely regional expressions that can be creatively manipulated: One often encounters the most bewildering varieties of styles in new traditional developments, particularly in the United States. There are Cycladic villages on the Californian coast; Orientalizing Shingle Style houses in upstate New York; Byzantine domes in South Carolina; Spanish Colonial buildings in the American Midwest; and so on. Before the emergence of eclecticism in the mid-eighteenth century, and unless they were actually constructed in different periods, buildings within particular cultural spheres of influence employed shared vocabularies of forms. These were derived from regional building and craft traditions, and borrowed classical expressions that had been absorbed and adapted locally over successive generations. Sometimes they were entirely imported but never without the societies that produced them in the first place; or, if an embedded immigrant community wished to preserve its familiar building types and expressions, these would be appropriately adapted to the regional craft traditions and employ available local materials and techniques. It was therefore natural for buildings to have strong affinities with each other, and their unique combinations of forms gave rise to what we call "styles." However carefully executed or refined contemporary traditional buildings may be in their details, if they do not build on established regional types they will appear capricious and misrepresent the cultures from which their expressions ultimately derive. As much as they may satisfy their owners' tastes, these kinds of projects tend to give credence to the argument that contemporary traditional architecture suffers from a paucity of ideas and is incapable of forging a distinctive approach of its own. Such an approach, of course, does exist, and it is a fundamentally regionalist one that needs to be reinforced at every level. Questions of authenticity also arise with buildings that cling too faithfully to remote historical types and cultural expressions, like those that dogged eclectic architects in the late nineteenth and early twentieth centuries, and which they failed to convincingly address. There is of course a spurious aspect to these concerns, as history shows that each generation will borrow liberally from previous periods and cultures, especially if the buildings they look to are permanent components of the urban fabric. The questions however serve to remind us of the importance of consistency in the use of architectural expressions and, above all, respect for local traditions and the ability to operate creatively within their formal parameters.

A resignation to the use of modern materials and constructional techniques. Despite the progress by new traditional architects in resuscitating neglected building arts, hardly anything remains of the crafts on which traditional architecture once depended. The rise of Modernism ensured that frame and curtain wall (or "exterior envelope") construction would become the exclusive approach in the assemblage of buildings. This has made it significantly more difficult, and costly, to construct traditional buildings properly, in many places downright impossible on account of ensconced building codes. This is despite the fact that well-built traditional masonry structures have a significantly longer life span than anything that the modern industry can produce, which is counted in centuries rather than decades: three hundred years instead of thirty, even more if a building is loved and cared for.[60] Premodern construction techniques not only produced enduring buildings, they also gave rise to the rich vocabulary of forms associated with classical and traditional architecture. The "tectonic" qualities of these architectural languages derive from their ability to reveal their origin in the techniques of straightforward, load-bearing construction.

Unfortunately most new traditional buildings do not employ the solid masonry walls that they want us to believe that they are made of. Costing and difficulty in procuring traditional materials and techniques have driven even the most conscientious new traditional architects to accept materials like reconstituted stone, exposed concrete, fiberglass, etc, and ephemeral contemporary techniques like cavity wall and steel and concrete frame construction. Telltale signs of "sham" traditional buildings are expansion joints, shallow window and door reveals, weep holes, and receding foundation walls. A host of mistakes can also be expected from construction crews unfamiliar with traditional techniques and building details; the most frequent and offensive of these errors are shallow lintels, missing archivolts, diminutive quoins, vertically stacked bricks in jack arches, insufficient masonry beneath cornices, etc. But even when the more fastidious designers take care to ensure proper detailing and disguise expansion joints and mistakes, the fact remains that the buildings that they have taken such pains to design and execute will be much shorter lived by comparison with older traditional examples.

Of the various areas of concern for new traditional architecture, this one is of central importance, on par with the promotion of a genuinely urban sensibility. If the questions of authenticity and the nature of formal expressions are to be effectively addressed, traditional architects must insist on employing traditional materials and solid, load-bearing constructional techniques, or at least adapting required frame construction to ensure self-supporting exterior walls.[61] The issue of costing needs to be understood not on the short-term scale of a fifteen- or thirty-year investment—which entails eventual replacement or maintenance and repair/restitution of buildings (hence deferred expenditures, renegotiation of loans, etc.)—but on a far more advantageous, long-term basis of greater initial cost of construction with minimal subsequent upkeep and repairs.

The argument for restituting traditional building techniques is strengthened by the ecological advantages of employing natural building materials. Unlike modernist buildings, which make primary use of imported synthetic and artificial products that are mined, cast, extruded, etc., and which tend to be toxic and/or hazardous to dispose of, traditional materials are locally available, friendly to the environment, and mostly reusable. In addition, their embodied energy is significantly lower than that of modern materials. Their inherently ecological and sustainable qualities make them far more desirable and advantageous than contemporary products. If the building industry and architectural profession can ever lay claim to an environmentally responsible outlook, it will be with the reintroduction and promotion of traditional building materials and techniques. Traditional architects cannot continue to yield and compromise on this fundamental issue.

There are, of course, many other matters to which new traditional architecture must tend; the concerns here outlined, however, need to be addressed decisively and without delay. The outcome depends ultimately on the intelligence and industry with which traditional architects, especially members of the current, emerging generation, will apply themselves over the next few decades. New classical and traditional architecture has everything a movement requires in order to achieve success: a finely crafted intellectual armature with a body of theoretical and realized work; a record of continual development and growth since its emergence some thirty years ago; a lineage that stretches back through history; enormous cultural diversity, expressed in the countless regional traditions around the world; schools and professional organizations committed to furthering its cause; and finally, a significant and ever-growing number of well-educated and dedicated young designers who have entered the professional arena armed with knowledge of architectural language, composition, precedent, and history. Most importantly, they have the benefit of cultural hindsight. Thus, while building on the lessons of the last three decades, they may avoid repeating the mistakes made by their predecessors. The work exhibited in this book is testimony to the strength of their vision as much as to their talent and commitment.

Endnotes

1. This essayist chooses to capitalize the terms Modernism, Modernist, etc., but not traditional, classical, new classical, etc. This is because the former represents a movement—hence the ending: "ism"—while the latter do not and are used as simple descriptive nouns.

2. The terms "new traditional" and "new classical" architecture are here used interchangeably; see Samir Younés's discussion in "Modern Traditional Architecture: Notes on an Intellectual Lineage."

3. Léon Krier, *Architecture and Urban Design 1967–1972*, ed. Richard Economakis (London: Academy Editions, 1992).

4. Demetri Porphyrios, *Classical Architecture* (London: Academy Editions, 1992).

5. Alan Greenberg, *The Architecture of Democracy* (New York: Rizzoli, 2006).

6. Robert Jan van Pelt and Carroll William Westfall, *Architectural Principles in the Age of Historicism* (New Haven, CT: Yale University Press, 1991).

7. David Watkin, A *History of Western Architecture* (London: Laurence King Publishing, 2005).

8. *Archives D'Architecture Moderne* 33 (Brussels: AAM, 1987).

9. Thanks in large part to the efforts of faculty members Thomas Norman Rajkovich and David Mayernik, both of whom apprenticed in Blatteau's office.

10. For instance the Oregon School of Design (1988–90) and the Universidade Católica Portguesa in Viseu, Portugal (2002–5).

11. John Simpson: *The Queen's Gallery Buckingham Palace and Other Works* (London: Papadakis Publisher, 2002); *New Classicists: Robert Adam and the Search for a Modern Classicism* (Mulgrave, Australia: Images Publishing, 2010); *Thomas Gordon Smith and the Rebirth of Classical Architecture* (London: Papadakis Publisher, 2001).

12. Elizabeth Meredith Dowling, *New Classicism: The Rebirth of Traditional Architecture* (New York: Rizzoli Publications, 2004).

13. The Institute of Classical Architecture, *A Decade of Art & Architecture 1992–2002* (New York: The Institute of Classical Architecture, 2002).

14. Alireza Sagharchi and Lucien Steil, *New Palladians: Modernity and Sustainability for 21st Century Architecture* (London: Artmedia Press, 2010).

15. These publications follow on earlier surveys like Alan Powers, ed., *Real Architecture: An Exhibition of Classical Buildings by the New Generation of Architects* (London: The Building Centre Trust: 1987); Robert A. M. Stern, *Modern Classicism* (New York: Rizzoli Publications, 1988); and Richard Economakis, ed., *Building Classical: A Vision of Europe and America* (1993).

16. Giacomo Barozzi da Vignola, *Canon of the Five Orders of Architecture*, trans. and commentary Branko Mitrović (Woodbridge, UK: Acanthus Press, 1999); Branko Mitrović, *Learning from Palladio* (New York: W. W. Norton & Co., 2004).

17. Ingrid D. Rowland and Thomas Noble Howe, *Vitruvius: Ten Books on Architecture* (Cambridge: Cambridge University Press, 1999).

18. Thomas Gordon Smith, *Vitruvius on Architecture* (New York: Monacelli Press, 2003).

19. Peter Pennoyer and Anne Walker, *The Architecture of Delano & Aldrich* (New York: W. W. Norton & Co., 2003); *The Architecture of Warren & Wetmore* (New York: W. W. Norton & Co., 2006); *The Architecture of Grosvenor Atterbury* (New York: W. W. Norton & Co., 2009).

20. Marc Appleton, *George Washington Smith: An Architect's Scrapbook* (Los Angeles: Tailwater Press, 2001).

21. Jeffrey Tilman, *Arthur Brown, Jr.: Progressive Classicist* (New York: W. W. Norton & Co., 2006).

22. *The Classicist*. 8 (2009).

23. Christine Franck, *José M. Allegue: A Builder's Legacy*, ed. Barbara M. Walker, (Lunenburg, VT: The Stinehour Press, 2002).

24. Jean-Baptiste Minnaert, *Pierre Barbe: Achitectures* (Paris: Institut Français d'Architecture, 1991).

25. Lucy Archer, *Raymond Erith: Progressive Classicist 1904–1973* (Albuquerque, NM: Cygnet Press, 1985).

26. William Chambers, *A Treatise on the Decorative Part of Civil Architecture* (Mineola, NY: Dover Publications, 2003).

27. Nathaniel Cortlandt Curtis, *The Secrets of Architectural Composition* (Mineola, NY: Dover Publications, 2011).

28. Arthur Stratton, *Form and Design in Classic Architecture* (Mineola, NY: Courier Dover Publications, 2004).

29. Johann Matthäus von Mauch and Charles-Pierre Joseph Normand, *Parallel of the Classical Orders* (Woodbridge, UK: Acanthus Press, 1998).

30. Georges Gromort, *The Elements of Classical Architecture*, ed. and introduction Henry Hope Reed (Woodbridge, UK: Acanthus Press, 1998).

31. C. Howard Walker, *Theory of Moldings* (New York: W. W. Norton & Co., 2007).

32. William R. Ware, *The American Vignola: A Guide to the Making of Classical Architecture* (Mineola, NY: Dover Publications, 1994).

33. Hector d'Espouy, *Greek and Roman Architecture in Classic Drawings* (Mineola, NY: Dover Publications, 1981).

34. The first "modern" (i.e., post-WWII) manual of this kind was Robert Chitham's *The Classical Orders of Architecture* (Oxford, UK: Elsevier Architectural Press, 1985; reprinted 2005).

35. Robert Adam, *Classical Architecture: A Comprehensive Handbook to the Tradition of Classical Style* (New York: Harry N. Abrams, 1991).

36. Steven W. Semes, *The Architecture of the Classical Interior* (New York: W. W. Norton & Co., 2004).

37. Jean-François Gabriel, *Classical Architecture for the Twenty-First Century: An Introduction to Design* (New York: W. W. Norton & Co., 2004).

38. Samir Younés, in *The True, the Fictive and the Real: The Historical Dictionary of Architecture of Quatremère de Quincy*, A. C. Quatremère de Quincy (London: Papadakis Publisher, 1999).

39. David Mayernik, *Timeless Cities: An Architect's Reflections on Renaissance Italy* (Boulder, CO: Westview Press, 2003).

40. Steven Semes, *The Future of the Past: A Conservation Ethic for Architecture, Urbanism, and Historic Preservation* (New York: W. W. Norton & Company, 2009).

41. Lykoudis is the Francis and Kathleen Rooney Dean of the School of Architecture.

42. Brian Hanson and Samir Younés, "Reuniting Urban Form and Urban Process: The Prince of Wales's Urban Design Task Force," *Journal of Urban Design* 6, no. 2 (2001).

43. This project, which was produced in the space of only ten days, received a 2010 CNU Award of Excellence.

44. See "2011 Charter Awards Winners Announced," *Better Cities & Towns*, April 19, 2011.

45. John Nagy, "The Rome of the Americas," *Notre Dame Magazine* (Winter 2011–12): 25–32. These well-publicized efforts have helped to break the long-held but patently false impression that Notre Dame shuns urbanism in favor of instruction in the classical language of architecture.

46. Recruitment of young classicists has been greatly facilitated by the recently instituted Career Fair at the School of Architecture of the University of Notre Dame in Indiana, which takes place yearly in the spring semester.

47. Marianne Cusato and Ben Pentreath with Richard Sammons and Léon Krier, *Get Your House Right: Architectural Elements to Use & Avoid* (New York: Sterling Publishing, 2007).

48. Stephen A. Mouzon with Susan M. Henderson, *Traditional Construction Patterns: Design & Detail Rules of Thumb* (New York: McGraw Hill, 2004).

49. See Ray Gindroz and Karen Levine, *The Architectural Pattern Book: A Tool for Building Great Neighborhoods* (New York: W. W. Norton & Co., 2004).

50. Hugh Pearman, "The History Boys," *RIBA Journal* (May 2010): 24–28.

51. Ibid., p. 28.

52. Veral Harlan Custom Furniture, co-owned by Harlan and designer Defne Veral.

53. Mohon-Imber interiors, based in Austin, Texas.

54. Barbara Opar, "Digital Collaborations Within and Beyond the Design Academy: The Library Transformed," *ACSA News* (April 2012).

55. James Packer and Gilbert Gorski, *The Roman Forum in the Age of the Emperors* (Cambridge: Cambridge University Press, forthcoming).

56. Paul Brenner, Douglas Thain, Amiee Buccellato, and David B. Go, "Environmentally Opportunistic Computing," in *Handbook of Energy-Aware and Green Computing*, eds. Ishfaq Ahmad and Sanjay Ranka (Baco Raton, FL: CRC Press, 2012).

57. Rollings received her undergraduate degree in architecture at the University of Notre Dame, and completed her doctoral dissertation at Cornell's College of Human Ecology in 2012.

58. Work by new traditional architects is not to be confused with pseudo-traditional creations by builders and designers who lack relevant professional or academic experience and credentials.

59. See David Brussat, "A New Classical Flower in Guatemala," *Architecture Here and There* (blog), *The Providence Journal*, February 2, 2012, http://blogs.providencejournal.com/ri-talks/architecture-here-there/2012/02/column-a-new-classical-flower-in-guatemala.html.

60. The issue of building longevity and the relative lifespan of buildings was discussed at the colloquium "Durability in Construction," held October 26–28, 2010, at the University of Notre Dame.

61. Two recent examples of this kind of construction are the new Whitman College at Princeton by Porphyrios Associates (2003), and the addition to Horace Trumbauer's Carhart Residence in Manhattan by John Simpson & Partners and Zivkovic Associates (2006).

Bibliographical Chronology

A selection compiled by Samir Younés.

Note: This selected bibliography includes books that influenced the formation of modern traditional architecture in a cross-cultural context since the early twentieth century. Books that have had one edition are listed in the original year of publication. Books that have had multiple editions have been listed in their latest edition. Only a few architectural treatises have been listed, given that the rich literature of the treatise is well known to traditional architects. This bibliography is intended to serve as a dossier for tracing a broad intellectual history.

1904 Guadet, Julien. *Eléments et théorie de l'architecture*, Paris: Librairie de la construction moderne.

1904 Gromort, Georges. *Choix d'éléments empruntés à l'architecture classique*. Paris: Vincent.

1915 *McKim, Mead & White Architects*. 4 vols. New York, Architectural Book Co.

1924 Scott, Geoffrey. *The Architecture of Humanism*. New York: Scribner.

1924 *The Architecture of John Russell Pope*. 3 vols. New York: Helburn.

1926–52 Lavedan, Pierre. *L'histoire de l'urbanisme*. Paris: Laurens.

1934 Mumford, Lewis. *Technics and Civilization*. New York: Harcourt Brace.

1936 Lovejoy, Arthur. *The Great Chain of Being*. Cambridge: Harvard University Press.

1938 Mumford, Lewis. *The Culture of Cities*. New York: Harcourt Brace.

1943 Choisy, Auguste. *L'histoire de l'architecture*. Paris: Baranger.

1959 Muratori, Saverio. *Studi per una operante storia urbana di Venezia*. 2 vols. Rome: Istituto poligrafico dello stato.

1960 Lynch, Kevin. *The Image of the City*. Cambridge: M.I.T.

1961 Jacobs, Jane. *The Death and Life of Great American Cities*. New York: Vintage Books.

1961 Mumford, Lewis. *The City in History*. New York: Harcourt Brace.

1963 Muratori, Saverio. *Studi per una operante storia urbana di Roma*. Rome: Consiglio nazionale delle ricerche.

1964 Ellul, Jacques. *The Technological Society* (1954, *La technique ou l'enjeu du siècle*). John Wilkinson, trans. New York: Vintage.

1965 *Camillo Sitte, City Planning According to Artistic Principles* (1889). George and Christine Collins, trans. New York: Random House.

1965 Choay, Françoise. *Urbanisme, utopies et* réalités. Paris: Seuil.

1965 Argan, Giulio Carlo. *Progetto e destino*. Milan: Il saggiatore.

1966 Aymonino, Carlo, Aldo Rossi, et al. *La città di Padova*. Rome: Oficina.

1966 Rossi, Aldo. *L'architettura della città*. Padua: Marsilio.

1967 Grassi, Giorgio. *La costruzione logica dell'architettura*. Padua: Marsilio.

1967 Bacon, Edmund. *Design of Cities*. New York: Viking Press.

1967–70 Mumford, Lewis. *The Myth of the Machine*. New York: Harcourt & Brace.

1968 Mumford, Lewis. *The Urban Prospect*. New York: Harcourt & Brace.

1968 Lefèbvre, Henri. *Le droit à la ville*. Paris: Ellipses.

1970 Baudrillard, Jean. *La société de consommation*. Paris: Denoël.

1971 Heidegger, Martin. *Poetry, Language, Thought*. Albert Hofstadter, trans. New York: Harper & Row.

1972 Desgodetz, Antoine. *Les édifices antiques de Rome* (1682). Portland, OR: Collegium Graphicum.

1973 Milizia, Francesco. *Principi dell'architettura civile* (1847). Milan: Majocchi.

1973 Fathy, Hassan. *Architecture for the Poor*. Chicago: University of Chicago Press.

1973 Ardalan, Nader, and Laleh Bakhtiar. *The Sense of Unity*. Chicago: University of Chicago Press.

1973 Bonfanti, E., R. Bonicalzi, A. Rossi, M. Scolari, D. Vitale. *Architettura Razionale*. Milano: Franco Angeli.

1973 Cervellati, P-L, and R. Scannavini. *Bologna: politica e metodologia nei centri storici*. Bologna: Il Mulino.

1975–90 *Archives d'architecture moderne* No. 1–40 (serial, having begun as a Bulletin d'informations).

1975 Aymonino, Carlo, et al. *Le città capitale del XIX° secolo*. Rome: Officina Edizioni.

1976 Wangerin, Gerda, Gerhard Weiss, and Steen Eiler Rasmussen. *Heinrich Tessenow, Baumeister, 1876-1950*. Essen, Germany: Bacht.

1977 Watkin, David. *Morality and Architecture*. Oxford: Clarendon.

1977 Bloomer, Kent, and Charles Moore. *Body, Memory, and Architecture*. New Haven: Yale.

1977 Drexler, Arthur. *The Architecture of L'Ecole des Beaux-Arts*. London: Secker & Warburg.

1977 Laugier, Marc-Antoine. *An Essay on Architecture* (1755). Los Angeles: Hennessey & Ingalls.

1977 Heidegger, Martin. *The Question Concerning Technology*. New York: Harper & Row.

1977 Alexander, Christopher, et al. *A Pattern Language*. New York: Oxford University Press.

1978 Rowe, Colin, and Fred Koetter. *Collage City*. Cambridge: M.I.T..

1978 Krier, Léon, Maurice Culot, eds. *Architecture rationelle: La reconstruction de la ville européenne*. Brussels: Archives d'architecture moderne.

1979 Krier, Rob. *Urban Space*. New York: Rizzoli.

1979 Delevoy, Robert, et al., eds. *La Cambre, 1928–1978*. Brussels: Archives d'architecture moderne.

1979 Graves, Michael, ed. *Roma Interrotta*. London: Architectural Design.

1979 Brasini, Luca, ed. *L'opera architettonica e urbanistica di Armando Brasini*. Rome.

1979 Scruton, Roger. *The Aesthetics of Architecture*. New Jersey: Princeton.

1980 Krier, Léon, Maurice Culot, eds. *Contre-projets, Counter-projects, Controprogetti*. Brussels: Archives d'architecture moderne.

1980 Panerai, Philippe, et al., eds. *Eléments d'analyse urbaine*. Brussels: Archives d'architecture moderne.

1980 Barey, André, ed. *Déclaration de Bruxelles*. Brussels: Archives d'architecture moderne.

1980 Quatremère de Quincy, Antoine Chrysostôme. *De l'imitation* (1823). Introductions by Léon Krier and Demetri Porphyrios. Brussels: Archives d'architecture moderne.

1980 Ellul, Jacques. *L'empire du non-sens*. Paris: Presses Universitaires de France.

1980 Ellul, Jacques. *The Technological System* (1977). Joachim Neugroschel, trans. New York: Continuum.

1980 Tatarkiewicz, Wladyslaw and Martinus Nijhoff. *A History of Six Ideas*. London: PWN, Polish scientific publishers.

1980 Norberg-Schulz, Christian. *Genius Loci: Towards a Phenomenology of Architecture*. New York: Rizzoli.

1980 *La presenza del passato*. Biennale di Venezia.

1980 Jencks, Charles, ed. *Post-modern Classicism: the new synthesis*. London: Architectural Design.

1980 Palladio, Andrea, Licisco Magagnato and Paola Marini. *I quattri libri* (1581). Milan: Il Polifilo.

1981 Porphyrios, Demetri, ed. *On the Methodology of Architectural History*. New York: St. Martin's Press.

1981 *Pompéi, travaux et envois* . . . Paris: École nationale supérieure des Beaux-Arts.

1981 Schinkel, Karl Friedrich. *Schinkel, Collection of Architectural Designs* . . . (1866). Chicago: Exedra Books.

1981 Rykwert, Joseph. *On Adam's House in Paradise*. Cambridge: M.I.T..

1981 *The Cornell Journal of Architecture* (serial No. 1–4). New York: Rizzoli distrib.

1981 Huet, Bernard. *Anachroniques d'architecture*. Brussels: Archives d'architecture moderne.

1982 Porphyrios, Demetri, ed. *Classicism Is Not a Style*. London: Papadakis.

1982 *Innocenzo Sabbatini, Architettura tra tradizione e rinnovamento, progetti: 1914–1940*. Rome: Architettura Arte Moderna.

1982 Letarouilly, Paul. *Edifices de Rome Moderne* (1840). New York: Princeton Architectural Press.

1982 *La Laurentine et l'invention de la villa romaine*. Institut français d'architecture. Paris: Editions le Moniteur.

1982 Portoghesi, Paolo. *After Modern Architecture*. New York: Rizzoli.

1982 Krier, Rob. *Urban projects, 1968–1982*. New York: Rizzoli.

1983 Portoghesi, Paolo. *Postmodern: the Architecture of the Post-Industrial Society*. New York: Rizzoli.

1983 Ledoux, Claude Nicolas. *L'architecture considérée* . . . (1847). New York: Princeton Architectural Press.

1983 Pérez-Gómez, Alberto. *Architecture and the Crisis of Modern Science*. Cambridge: M.I.T.

1983 Geist, Johann Friedrich. *Arcades*. Cambridge: M.I.T.

1984 Krier, Léon. *Houses, Palaces, and Cities*. London: Academy Editions.

1984 Porphyrios, Demetri, ed. *Building and Rational Architecture*. London: Academy Editions.

1984 Linasazoro, José Ignazio. *Le projet classique en architecture*. Brussels: Archives d'architecture moderne.

1984 Alphand, Adolphe. *Les promenades de Paris* . . . (1867-1873). New York: Princeton Architectural Press.

1985 *I terreni della tipologia*, Casabella, January–February. Milan: Electa periodici.

1985 Gruber, Karl. *Forme et caractère de la ville allemande* (1952). Brussels: Archives d'architecture moderne.

1985 *Roma antiqua, Forum, Colisée, Palatin*. Paris: Ecole nationale supérieure des Beaux-Arts.

1985 *The Charlottesville Tapes*. New York: Rizzoli.

1985 Archer, Lucy. *Raymond Erith, Architect*. Oxfordshire, England: Cygnet.

1986 Dennis, Michael. *Court and Garden*. Cambridge: M.I.T.

1986 Hellman, Marie-Christine, Philippe Fraisse, and Annie Jacques, eds. *Paris, Rome, Athènes*. Paris: École nationale supérieure des Beaux-Arts.

1986 Fathy, Hassan, Walter Shearer and Abdel Rahman Ahmed Sultan, eds. *Natural Energy and Vernacular Architecture*. Chicago: University of Chicago Press.

1986 Durand, Jean-Nicolas-Louis. *Recueil et parallèle des edifices de tout genre* . . . (1800). Nördinghen, Germany: A. Uhl.

1986 Shepherd, John, and Geoffrey Jellicoe. *Italian Gardens of the Renaissance* (1925). New York: Princeton Architectural Press.

1987 Krier, Rob. *Amiens, La reconstruction du centre historique*. Brussels: Archives d'architecture moderne.

1987 Steil, Lucien, ed. *Tradition and Architecture*. London: Academy Editions.

1987 Rotthier, Philippe. *Architectures Ibiza*. Brussels: Archives d'architecture moderne.

1988 Krier, Rob. *Elements of Architecture*. New York: Rizzoli.

1988 Hegemann, Werner, and Elbert Peets. *Civic Art: The American Vitruvius* (1922). New York: Princeton Architectural Press.

1988 Papadakis, Andreas, ed. *The New Classicism in Architecture and Urbanism*. London: Academy Editions.

1988 Cenicacelaya, Javier, and Inigo Salona, eds. *Composición arquitectonica* (serial, beginning in 1988). Bilbao, Spain: El Instituto.

1988 Smith, Thomas G. *Classical Architecture, Rule and invention*. Layton, UT: Peregrine Smith.

1988 Breitman, Marc, and Maurice Culot, eds. *La goutte d'or, Faubourg de Paris*. Brussels: Archives d'architecture moderne.

1988 *Alberti: On the Art of Building in Ten Books*. Joseph Rykwert, Neil Leach, and Robert Tavernor, trans. Cambridge: M.I.T.

1988 Hersey, George. *The Lost Meaning of Classical Architecture*. Cambridge: M.I.T.

1989 H.R.H., The Prince of Wales. *A Vision of Britain*. New York: Doubleday.

1989 Ansay, Pierre, and René Schoonbrodt, eds. *Penser la ville*. Brussels: Archives d'architecture moderne.

1989 *The Four Elements of Architecture* (1851). Gottfried Semper, Harry Mallgrave, and Wolfgang Hermann, trans. New York: Cambridge University Press.

1989 Goy, Richard. *Venetian Vernacular Architecture*. New York: Cambridge University Press.

1991 Adam, Robert. *Classical Architecture*. New York: Abrams.

1991 Duany, Andrés, and Elizabeth Platter-Zyberk. *Towns and Town making Principles*. Alex Krieger and William Lennertz, eds. New York: Rizzoli.

1991 Van Pelt, Robert Jan, and Carroll William Westfall. *Architectural Principles in the Age of Historicism*. New Haven: Yale.

1991 Minnaert, Jean-Baptiste. *Pierre Barbe. Architectures*. Liège: Mardaga.

1992 Porphyrios, Demetri. *Classical Architecture, The Living Tradition*. New York: McGraw-Hill.

1992 Economakis, Richard, ed. *Léon Krier, Architecture and Urban Design, 1967-92*. London: Academy Editions.

1992 Tagliaventi, Gabriele, and Liam O'Connor, eds. *A Vision of Europe: Architecture and Urbanism for the European city*. Florence: Alinea.

1992 *Roma antiqua, Grandi edifici pubblici*. Rome: Edizioni carte segrete.

1992 Papadakis, Andreas, ed. *Paternoster Square and the New Classical Tradition*. London: Academy Editions.

1992 Curl, James Steven. *Classical Architecture*. New York: Van Nostrand Reinhold.

1993 Economakis, Richard, ed. *Building Classical: A Vision of Europe and America*. London: Academy Editions.

1993 HRH The Prince of Wales. *Architecture and the Environment*. Andreas Papadakis, ed. London: Architectural Design.

1993 Economakis, Richard, ed. *Architecture in Arcadia*. London: Academy Editions.

1993 Economakis, Richard, et al., eds. *Interventions in Historic Centres*. London: Academy Editions.

1993 *Quinlan Terry: Selected Works*. London: Academy Editions.

1993 Krečič, Peter. *Plecnik. The Complete Works*. New York: Whitney Library of Design.

1993 Burnham, Daniel. *The Plan of Chicago* (1908). New York: Princeton Architectural Press.

1993 Katz, Peter. *The New Urbanism*. New York: McGraw-Hill.

1993 Yampolsky, Mariana. *The Traditional Architecture of Mexico*. New York: Thames & Hudson.

1994 Tagliaventi, Gabriele, ed. *Città Giardino*. Rome: Gangemi.

1994 Tagliaventi, Gabriele, ed. *Archi e Colonne* (serial, beginning in 1993).

1994 *The Classicist* (serial, beginning in 1994). New York: The Institute for Classical Architecture.

1995 Crowe, Norman. *Nature and the Idea of a Man-Made World*. Cambridge: M.I.T.

1995 Scruton, Roger. *The Classical Vernacular*. New York: St. Martin's Press.

1995 Chitham, Robert. *The Classical Order in Architecture*. London: Elsevier.

1995 Greenberg, Allan. *Allan Greenberg Selected Works*. London: Academy Editions.

1996 Tagliaventi, Gabriele, ed. *A Vision of Europe: Urban Renaissance*. Bologna: Grafis.

1996 Kuntsler, James H. *Home from Nowhere*. New York: Simon & Schuster.

1996 Viollet-le-Duc, Eugène-Emmanuel. *Encyclopédie medieval* (1868). Georges Bernage, ed. Tours, France: Inter-Livres.

1996 Grossman, Elizabeth. *The Civic Art of Paul Cret*. New York: Cambridge University Press.

1996 Serlio, Sebastiano, Vaughan Hart, and Peter Hicks, eds. *Tutte le opere d'architettura*. New Haven, Yale University Press.

1997 Zucconi, G., ed. *Gustavo Giovannoni, Dal capitello alla città*. Milan.

1997 Giovanetti, Francesco, ed. *Manuale del recupero del comune di Roma*. Rome: DEI.

1997 Marconi, Paolo. *Manuale del recupero del centro storico di Palermo*. Francesco Giovanetti, ed. Palermo: Flaccovio.

1998 Krier, Léon. *Architecture, Choice or Fate*. Kilbees Farm, England: Papadakis.

1998 Giovanetti, Francesco, ed. *Manuale del recupero del comune di Città di Castello*. Rome: DEI.

1998 Hanson, Brian, and Lucien Steil, eds. *The Potsdam Project*. The Prince of Wales's Urban Design Task Force.

1999 Caniggia, Gianfranco, and G. Luigi Maffei. *Composizione architettonica e tipologia edilizia*. 2 vols. Venice: Marsilio.

1999 Economakis, Richard, Norman Crowe, and Michael Lykoudis, eds. *Building Cities*. London: Artmedia.

1999 Younés, Samir. *The True, the Fictive, and the Real. The Historical Dictionary of Architecture of A-C, Quatremère de Quincy* (1832). London: Papadakis.

2000 Tagliaventi, Gabriele, ed. *L'altra modernità, 1900–2000*. Savona: Dogma.

2000 Duany, Andrés, Elizabeth Platter-Zyberk, and Jeff Speck. *Suburban Nation*. New York: North Point Press.

2000 Durand, Jean-Nicholas-Louis. *Précis des leçons d'architecture . . .* (1802–05). Los Angeles: Getty.

2001 Kuntsler, James H. *The City in Mind*. New York: Free Press.

2001 John, Richard. *Thomas Gordon Smith and the Rebirth of Classical Architecture*. London: Papadakis.

2002 John, Richard, and David Watkin. *John Simpson*. London: Papadakis.

2002 Younés, Samir, ed. *Ara Pacis controprogetti*. Florence: Alinea.

2002 Jacques, Annie, Stéphane Verget, and Catherine Virlouvet. *Italia antiqua, Envois de Rome. . . .* Paris: Ecole nationale supérieure des Beaux-Arts.

2003 McEwen, Indra Kagis. *Vitruvius. Writing the Body of Architecture*. Cambridge: M.I.T.

2003 Mayernik, David. *Timeless Cities*. Boulder, CO: Westview Press.

2003 Mitrovič, Branko, Rau Hoskins, and Carin Wilson, eds. *Traditional Architecture*. Auckland, New Zealand: School of Architecture.

2003–07 *The Richard Driehaus Prize: Léon Krier, Demetri Porphyrios, Quinlan Terry, Allan Greenberg, Jacquelin Robertson*. Nortre Dame, IN: University of Notre Dame, School of Architecture.

2004 Gabriel, Jean-François. *Classical Architecture for the 21st Century*. New York: Norton.

2004 Jacobs, Jane. *Dark Age Ahead*. New York: Random House.

2004 Mazzola, Ettore. *Controstoria dell'architettura moderna, 1900–1940*. Florence: Alinea.

2004 Semes, Steve. *The Architecture of the Classical Interior*. New York: Norton.

2004 Mitrović, Branko, *Learning from Palladio*. New York: Norton.

2004 Florio, Riccardo. *Origini e permanenze della classicità in architettura*. Rome: Officina.

2004 *Traditional Town Planning and Architecture*. Carmel, CA: International Making Cities Livable Council.

2005 Kuntsler, James H. *The Long Emergency*. New York: Atlantic Monthly Press.

2006 Greenberg, Allan *The Architecture of Democracy*. New York: Rizzoli.

2006 Krier, Rob. *Townspaces*. Basel: Birkhäuser.

2006 Hewitt, Mark, et al., eds. *Carrère & Hastings Architects*. New York: Acanthus Press.

2006 Miers, Mary. *American Houses: The Architecture of Fairfax & Sammons*. New York: Rizzoli.

2006 Lovelock, James. *The Revenge of Gaia*. Santa Barbara, CA: Allen Lane.

2008 Krier, Léon. *The Architectural Tuning of Settlements*. London: The Prince's Foundation for the Built Environment.

2008 Bontempi, Pier Carlo. *Piazza Nuova*. Bussels: Archives d'Architecture Moderne.

2008 Adam, Robert, and Matthew Hardy, eds. *Tradition Today*. Southampton, England: WIT.

2009 Krier, Léon. *The Architecture of Community*. Washington, D.C.: Island Press.

2009 Hardy, Matthew, ed. *The Venice Charter Revisited*. Newcastle, England: Cambridge Scholars.

2009 Lovelock, James. *The Vanishing Face of Gaia*. Santa Barbara, CA: Allen Lane.

2010 HRH The Prince of Wales. *Harmony*. New York: Harper-Collins.

2010 Sagharchi, Alireza, and Lucien Steil, eds. *The New Palladians*. London: Artmedia.

2010 Locher, Mira. *Traditional Japanese Architecture*. Rutland, VT: Tuttle.

2010 Thadani, Dhiru. *The Language of Towns and Cities*. New York: Rizzoli.

2010 Campbell, David. *Wood in Traditional Architecture*. Atglen, PA: Schiffer.

2010 Campbell, David. *Stone in Traditional Architecture*. Atglen, PA: Schiffer.

2011 Duany, Andrés, and DPZ. *Agrarian Urbanism*. London: The Prince's Foundation for the Built Environment.

2011 Fergusson, Mark. *New Traditional Architecture: Fergusson & Shamamian Architects*. New York: Rizzoli.

2011 Mitrović, Branko. *Philosophy for Architects*. New York: Princeton Architectural Press.

2012 Younés, Samir. *The Imperfect City: On Architectural Judgment*. London: Ashgate.

2012 Steil, Lucien, ed. *The Architectural Capriccio. Memory, Fantasy, and Invention*. London: Ashgate.

2013 Dowling, Elizabeth Meredith. *Michael Imber: Ranches, Villas, and Houses*. New York: Rizzoli.

2013 Thadani, Dhiru, ed. *Visions of Seaside*. New York: Rizzoli.

Illustration Credits

Courtesy Léon Krier—pp. 10–14, 20, 26 bottom, 28, 34 bottom
Courtesy Giancarlo Cataldi—p. 22 top right
Courtesy Arduino Cantàfora—p. 22 bottom
Courtesy Maurice Culot—p. 25
Courtesy Steven Peterson—p. 33
Courtesy Samir Younés—p. 34 top
Ada Hotel: Aga Khan Trust for Culture—pp. 40–41
Almeria Row: DLGV Architects & Urbanists—pp. 42–43
Altanella Di Villa Canali: Courtesy Pier Carlo Bontempi Architects—pp. 44–45
Amankora: Tanuj Goenka—p. 46 top; Shinkenchiku-Sha—p. 46 bottom, p. 47
Artklass Abandoibarra: Aitor Ortiz—pp. 50–51
Arts & Crafts House: Paul Graham—pp. 52–53
A'Samaliah Island: Aga Khan Trust for Culture—pp. 54–55
Auditorium Hall of NJU: Courtesy Atelier Zhao Chen—pp. 56–57
The Bachenheimer Building: Treve Johnson Photography
Bahrain Residence: R. Manzano Arquitectos—pp. 60–61
Bass Library at Yale University: Timothy Hursley—pp. 62–63
A Bath House: Paul Highnam—pp. 64–65, pp. 66–67
Belhaven – A New Beach Village: Courtesy Duncan McRoberts Associates—pp. 68–69
Bermuda Village: © Duany Plater-Zyberk & Co. / Photography by Carlos Morales—p. 70, p. 71 top left, p. 71 bottom; © Duany Plater-Zyberk & Co.—p. 71 top right
Caimitillo House: Photography by Luis Eduardo Guillen—pp. 72–73
Calabasa Civic Center: Peter Aaron / Esto—pp. 74–75
Caliza Pool: Jack Gardner Photography—pp. 76–77, p. 77 bottom; © Tommy Crow—p. 77 top
Campo Sano Village: Duany Plater-Zyberk & Co. / Photography by Paul Pedroso—p. 78, p. 79 center, p. 79 bottom; Duany Plater-Zyberk & Co. / Photography by Carlos Morales—p. 79 top
Can Miquel Roig: © Editorial TEHP—pp. 80–81
Cape Dutch House: Ariela Grossman—pp. 82–83
Carnegie Hill Brownstone: Peter Pennoyer Architects / Photography by Scott Frances and Jonathan Wallen—pp. 84–85
Casa de Las Lomas: Courtesy Jon D. McDonald—pp. 86–87
Casa Veloso Matas: Jose Cornelio da Silva—p. 88 top and bottom
Casa Sirena: Marco Corsetti—p. 89
Casa Do Médico: FG+SG Fotografia de Arquitectura—pp. 90–91
New Town of Cayalá: Designed by Richard Economakis / Photograph by Vicente Aguirre—p. 93 top; photograph by Vicente Aguirre—pp. 94–95, p. 96 top, p. 97 top; designed by Pedro Godoy and Maria Sanchez, rendering by Estudio Urbano—p. 96 center; fountain by Léon Krier, photograph by Vicente Aguirre—p. 96 bottom
Central Library: © J. Ghazbanpoor/Aga Khan Award for Architecture—pp. 98–99
Chalet in the Alps: Jose Da Silva of "ima'in Courchevel"—pp. 100–101; Todhunter Earle—102–3
Charlottenpalais: XIGN Movement for Patzchke—pp. 104–5
Churchill Court: Paul Redman—pp. 106–7
Citadel Broekpolder: Archive KK Architects—pp. 108–9
Cockerill Building: Mulhern+Steil—p. 110
Coral Gables Museum: Carlos Domenech Fine Art Photography—p. 111
Cotswold Residence: Courtesy Yiangou Architects—pp. 112–13
New Country House: Courtesy Nigel Anderson ADAM Architecture—pp. 114–15
Courthouse and Federal Building: Timothy Hursley—pp. 116–17
Danube Delta Eco Resort: Courtesy Stanhope Gate Architecture—pp. 120–23
De Haan, The New Concession: Maurice Culot – Arcas Paris—pp. 124–25
Dos Flores: Kurt Lischka, Moon Creek Studios—pp. 126–27
Drumlin Hall: Peter Pennoyer Architects / Photography by Scott Frances and Jonathan Wallen—128–29
Dupont Hall, University of Delaware: © Robert Lautman—p. 130 top, p. 131; © Thomas Noble—p. 130 bottom
Eau Chien: Peter Aaron / OTTO—p. 132 top right, p. 132 bottom, p. 133 top; Kegan Marshall—p, 132 top left, p. 133 bottom
Ecole Anatole France: Courtesy Breitman-Breitman—pp. 134–35
El Valle Residence: Luis Eduardo Guillen—pp. 136–37
Field Farm Village: John Critchley—pp. 138–39
Fine House: Carlos Morales Photography—pp. 140–41
Forest of Bere House: Courtesy Julian Bicknell & Associates—pp. 142–143
Frick Residence: Courtesy Alvin Holm Architects—p. 144
Gaia Building: Keith Baker—p. 145
Georgian House: Evan Joseph—pp. 146–47
Gorinchem Development: Scala Architecten—pp. 148–49
Granada Court: © Moule & Polyzoides, Architects and Urbanists—pp. 150–151
Halawa House: Courtesy Abdel-Wahed El-Wakil—p. 152
Hanover Lodge: Francis Terry—p. 154; June Buck—p. 155, pp. 156–57
Hertfordshire Country House: Chris Draper—pp. 158–59
Houses: Lisa Romerein—p. 160; Scott Francis / OTTO—p. 161
House on Scottish Island: Chris Draper—pp. 162–63
Houses in Toorak: Christopher Doyle Architects—pp. 164–67
Howard Theatre, Downing College: Nick Carter—p. 168 top and bottom; Courtesy Quinlan & Francis Terry Architects—p. 169 top and bottom
Immaculate Conception Church: © Hester + Hardaway Photographers—pp. 170–71
Indian Creek Residence: DLGV Architects & Urbanists
Janzon Residence: Jackie Arias Photography—pp. 174–75
Kadre Residence: Carlos Domenech Fine Art Photography—pp. 176–77
Kensington Palace, London, England: Andreas von Einsiedel © John Simpson Architects, LLP—pp. 178–79
La Colina: Photograph by Fritz von der Schulenburg © Bunny Williams¬—pp. 180¬–81
Lady Margaret Hall: Andreas von Einsiedel © John Simpson Architects, LLP—pp. 182–83
Lakeside, Specialist Care Home: Rob Currie—pp. 184–85
La Manzana: R. Manzano Arquitectos—pp. 186–87
Lehman Residence: Tony Soluri Photography—pp. 188–89
Levin Residence: Carlos Domenech Fine Art Photography—pp. 190–91
Mansion House: Courtesy Ivan Kniazev and Alexander Stepanov
Marbella Houses: Courtesy Donald Gray—pp. 194–95
Apartments in Mayfair: Nabeel Shehadah—pp. 196–97
McCormick Residence: Martinez & Alvarez Architects—p. 198; Gil Jacobs Photography—p. 199
Mediterranean House: Jack Gardner Photography—pp. 200–01
Messila Residence: Apache Photography—pp. 202–3
Montenmedio: R. Manzano Arquitectos—pp. 204–5, top and bottom
Mud House in Mudrapur: Aga Khan Trust for Culture—pp. 206–7
Museum at Odrinhas, Archaeological Museum and Arts and Crafts School: Courtesy ACN & AMB, LDA—p. 208, top, bottom left, bottom right
Netia Piercy House: Aga Khan Trust for Culture—p. 209
New Residences: Courtesy Fairfax & Sammons
New Cotswold House: Courtesy Yiangou Architects—pp. 212–13
Newham: Russell Taylor—pp. 214–15
Ningboshi Cichengzheng: Courtesy Atelier Zhao Chen—pp. 216–17
North Squad Residential and Academic Complex: Francis Dzikowski / Esto—pp. 218–21
Obrechtstraat: Photo Scala Architecten—p. 212
Ocean Course Clubhouse: Peter Aaron / Esto—p. 223, top and bottom
Our Lady of Guadalupe Seminary and Chapel of Saints Peter and Paul: Alan McIntyre Smith—pp. 224–27
Primary School and Community Centre: Aga Khan Trust for Culture—pp. 228–30
Princess Square: Courtesy Julian Bicknell & Associates—pp. 232–33
Promontory Pointe: Courtesy Michael Imber Architects
Punta Cana Church: Courtesy Ernesto Buch
Quiblatain Mosque: Courtesy Abdel-Wahed El-Wakil—pp. 238–39
Richard Green Gallery: Morley von Sternberg—pp. 240–41
Riva Development: Courtesy Breitman-Breitman—pp. 242–43
River Oaks Boulevard Garden Pavilion: © Hester + Hardaway Photographers—pp. 244–45
Rue St. Vincent: Rita Wolff—p. 246; Lucien Steil—p. 247
Saffrin Residence: Shigley Photo, Chicago—pp. 248–49
Sales Center: Jack Gardner Photography—pp. 250–51
Scheessele House: © Tim Buchman—p. 252
School in Rudrapur: Aga Khan Trust for Culture—pp. 254–55
Seaside Residence: Courtesy Leo Casas
September 11th Memorial: Russell Taylor—pp. 258–59
Sidi Bou Said Houses: Aga Khan Trust for Culture—pp. 260–61
South Main: James Dougherty – Dover, Kohl & Partners—pp. 262–63
St. Albans School: Ron Blount—p. 264; Celia Pearson—p. 265
Saint Margaret Mary Church: © Duncan G. Stroik—p. 266
Saint Theresa Education Center: © Mark Scheyer Photography—p. 267
St. Edward's Chapel, Casady School: Chris Landsberger—p. 268; Michael Ortega and Associates Photography—p. 269 top; John Daughtry / LOF Productions © 2009—p. 269 bottom
St. Erik Crescent: Courtesy Brunnberg & Forshed Arkitektkontor—p. 270
Summer Palace: Architects Ivan Kniazev, Irina Efendieva, Galina Sokolova / Photograph by Ivan Srokin © Ivan Kniazev—p. 271
't Haegsch Hof, Rivierenbuurt: Archive KK Architects—pp. 272–273
The American School in Switzerland: Michele Kestenholz—pp. 274, 275 top; Lorenzo Mussi—p. 275 bottom
The Palladium: Steve Hall © Hedrich Blessing—p. 277–79
The Villa: copyright © James McDonald 2012—pp. 280–83
Tommy Hilfiger Flagship Store: © Michael Biondo—pp. 284–85
Tottenham Court Road: Nick Carter—p. 287
Touma House: Aga Khan Trust for Culture—pp. 288–89
Tree House: Seth Harry & Associates—pp. 290–91
Villa Boim, Monte Da Herdade Do Rego: FG+SG Fotografia de Arquitectura—pp. 292–93
Villa Borelli: Courtesy Pier Carlo Bontempi Architects—pp. 294–95
Villa Gemma: Courtesy Luigi del Sordo—pp. 296–97
Villas in Germany: Courtesy Hans Kollhoff Architekten—p. 298 top, bottom
William Wake House: John Critchley—pp. 300–01
Whittlebury Lodge: Courtesy Peregrine Bryant—pp. 302–3
Wyatt Residence: Courtesy Alvin Holm Architects—pp. 304–5
Yakup Içgören House: Aga Khan Trust for Culture—pp. 306–7
Courtesy Richard M. Economakis—p. 310